Morning Meditations

Morning Meditations

DAILY REFLECTIONS TO AWAKEN
YOUR POWER TO CHANGE

Expert Life Advice From

Health and Wellness Professionals

EDITED BY

NORTON PROFESSIONAL BOOKS

W. W. Norton & Company
New York · London

For information about permission to reproduce selections from
this book, write to Permissions, W. W. Norton & Company, Inc.,
500 Fifth Avenue, New York, NY 10110

For information about special discounts for bulk purchases,
please contact W. W. Norton Special Sales at
specialsales@wwnorton.com or 800-233-4830

Manufacturing by Edwards Brothers Malloy, Ann Arbor
Book design by Molly Heron
Production manager: Leeann Graham

Library of Congress Cataloging-in-Publication Data

Morning meditations : daily reflections to awaken your power
to change : expert life advice from health and wellness professionals /
edited by Norton Professional Books. — First edition.
pages cm
Includes bibliographical references and index.
ISBN 978-0-393-70946-9 (hardcover)
1. Meditation. 2. Self-realization. 3. Reflection (Philosophy)
I. W.W. Norton & Company.
BF637.M4M67 2014
158.1'28—dc23
2014010470

W. W. Norton & Company, Inc.
500 Fifth Avenue, New York, N.Y. 10110
www.wwnorton.com

W. W. Norton & Company Ltd.
Castle House, 75/76 Wells Street, London W1T 3QT

1 2 3 4 5 6 7 8 9 0

Contents

Note to Readers

CULLED FROM THE leading therapeutic minds of our time, this pocket guide carefully compiles thought-provoking selections from a number of significant mental wellness books into a single, portable resource. Each entry offers a poignant life lesson, a strategy worth considering, or a way to think differently; all suggest a path to personal growth. A veritable therapist in your back pocket, this book contains passages that are designed to encourage, motivate, illuminate, expand, and support you in your daily life.

Following each excerpt are italicized suggestions, questions, or specific exercises to prompt further reflection, all intended to reinforce and expand upon the ideas featured in the entries.

Depending on your mood, you may wish to pick up the book and read only the passages themselves; at other times, you may want to dig a bit deeper and consider the questions or exercises posed. Use them as you wish.

The entries touch upon the following general themes:

Mindfulness
Self-Awareness
Change
Family
Relationships
Gratitude
Stress
Health
Forgiveness
Communication
Problem Solving
Goals

Selections may be read sequentially or thematically. Note that at the top of each entry is a label stating its predominant theme. As you read through the entries, you may find that one theme speaks to you more than another. If you wish to consult only those passages having to do with relationships, for example, refer to the thematic listing, by page number, at the back of the book. Many of the entries fit more than one theme, though only one theme is identified for each entry.

At the end of the book is another section of entries that offers guided visualizations and meditations. More focused and instructional than the other passages, these exercises are designed to teach basic meditation and relaxation skills.

Whether you are in search of a daily program for self-improvement and inspiration or are looking for a book to dip into when the spirit moves you, the selections here will provide you with profound yet practical starting points for further exploration.

A final note, the word "meditation" is used throughout in its most basic meaning—to contemplate, think about, mull over. Adherence to a specific meditative or religious practice is by no means required to use this book.

Remember that "First and foremost, meditation is an experience. The experience is so highly valued that it is considered an inward 'art.' Though the meditator returns to the center within the self, paradoxically he or she may transcend the limitations imposed on the self. So we invite you to empty your cup and enter the experience of meditation. There may you make new discoveries that will carry you through the therapeutic seas to a life of happiness and fulfillment."

Morning Meditations

General Meditations

Mindfulness

MEDITATION IS A time for sitting quietly, seemingly doing nothing. In the empty moment, meditation can be discovered. To Westerners, sitting quietly and doing nothing is often seen as a waste of time. How can anything significant be accomplished by doing nothing? Or is it really doing nothing? The answers to these questions require a shift in perspective. When people are willing to experiment with this shift, a new world of possibility may open up. Meditation is a tool for experiencing clearly, resulting in a direct and immediate link between thought and action. What seems at first to be a non-activity is in fact its own kind of activity.

Take a moment to reflect on the reasons why you bought this book. How do you plan to use it to change your daily experience of life? Are you willing to make a commitment to work with the pages of this book to examine your life and be open to changing it?

Self-Awareness

WHAT WE CALL an emotion is important, because the label we give it tells us how to handle the feeling and what action to take. For example, if we label an emotion as fear, we will look hurriedly around to find out what may be dangerous, and because we call it fear we will look for a way to protect ourselves or run away. On the other hand, if we label an emotion as anger our whole temperament will change. We will look out sternly to see who it is that has caused our anger. Instead of running away, we will angrily approach the person and demand that they stop. If we label an emotion as a higher state of emotional arousal caused by the fact that we drank 10 cups of coffee, we won't do anything about it; we won't run away or attack. Instead, we will stop drinking coffee, take time to relax, and wait for the stimulant to wear off.

Therefore, it is very important that we label an emotion correctly, because the name we bestow upon it tells us precisely what to do about it.

In this way our emotions are like another sense, like seeing, hearing, smelling, or tasting, all of which tell us about the world. The other senses tell us about the outside environment. Our emotions are an inner sense that tells us what is happening inside of us.

Try articulating your emotions to yourself as you feel them. Are you as precise about what you are feeling as you think you are? Can you make an effort to be really, really precise about what you feel and what may have caused it? Does recognizing the origin of an emotion and identifying it precisely make it seem more manageable?

Stress

CRISES CAN ALSO serve as wake-up calls. Many people tend to live life by inertia. You will continue on the path you are on, usually set by your family of origin, your culture, and early decisions unless something gets you to reexamine the direction you are taking. Crises can give you the time and opportunity to change course or recommit to an earlier abandoned dream.

Take some time to think about a crisis you have faced in your life. Now that it is in the past, can you see how this crisis provided you with any gifts? Any strengths? How did your view of the world change after coming out on the other side?

Family

THE ROLES OF each person can be thought of as organizationally stemming from an above, below, or beside position. Each person within a family may, at different times, be in each position. For example, parents are being parents when they are in the above (taking care of) role. On the other hand, a parent may choose to be in a beside role (as when being a model with a child and listening to the child). A parent may also choose to be in the below role (as when learning from children).

Individuals who only know how to be in one of the three roles limit the possibility for personal growth and development. It is important, for example, for parents to learn from their children how to have fun. It is also important for children to learn from their parents how to be responsible. It is through appreciating the differing roles of children and adults in a family that each person's life is enhanced and developing a stronger, healthier family is made possible.

Which position do you tend to slip into most easily with your family? Try taking on a role that comes less naturally to you today. What did you learn from that experience? If the experience was a positive one, try to incorporate some flexibility in the role you assume and notice the difference this makes.

Communication

A CONVERSATION REQUIRES each person to know how to speak up as well as how to listen. Healthy interpersonal interaction requires the ability to listen to others. There is, however, a difference between listening and hearing.

In Spanish, two totally separate words are used to differentiate between hearing and listening: *oír* and *escuchar*. The word *oír* refers to simply hearing sounds or spoken words. We may hear (*oír*) something or someone when conversation is not involved. For example, we may *oír* a door creaking or the words a person is saying without fully understanding the meaning behind the words or sounds. On the other hand when we listen to (*escuchar*) someone, we go beyond hearing to actually understanding the depth of the words' meaning, the feelings or intent of the message, and the energy level of the person speaking. To listen to another person is to make an important and intimate connection with that other person, even if we disagree with them.

⌒⌒ *The next time you find yourself in a tense conversation, pause to ask yourself whether you are really listening to the words that are being spoken, rather than merely hearing them and waiting to speak. Make a conscious effort in this situation to listen for understanding.*

Alternatively, reflect back on a recent difficult conversation. Did you participate as someone who really listened, *or just as someone who* heard? *How might the conversation have gone differently if you* listened *as* well *as* heard?

Self-Awareness

HELPING IS PART of the fabric of everyday living and it is one of the ways that we strengthen bonds between family and friends, our neighbors, those in our community, and even people we do not know but whom we help through charitable organizations. Helping also extends to animals, plants, our environment, and our world. We also help ourselves. Evidence for this is in the "self-help" movement. As you read this book, you are helping yourself feel happier and healthier.

Say to yourself: I belong to a great network of giving and receiving help. In reading my morning meditation, I am intentionally strengthening my bond with myself. In so doing, I am strengthening my bonds to my community.

Today, make a conscious effort to be helpful whenever possible. Notice the benefits you receive when extending yourself to others.

Problem Solving

I F YOU ARE worried about making mistakes you become anxious. If you are critical of yourself for making mistakes you tend to be depressed. If you believe others shouldn't make mistakes you become angry.

We've all heard the phrase *ready, aim, fire,* but the reality check is *ready, fire, aim.* This latter phrase is used as a mainstay of improv, where spontaneity is the goal. It is also real life, where we learn and develop solutions from trial and error. Mistakes are what we can determine only after the fact. We take the best action we can, see what happens next, and adjust, because the outcome is out of our control.

This is part of the creative process, the tinkering that comes as we get feedback about what works and what doesn't, whether it be the experience at the party, the conversation with our spouse, the design of a new fashion line. This perspective is found in the well-known inspirational quotation, "Good decisions come from experience, and experience comes from making bad decisions."

Think about a recent situation where, looking back on it, you realize you made a mistake. Can you learn anything from this experience? How will you apply the lessons learned from that event to something else?

Relationships

E MOTIONAL MATURITY IS a measure of the extent to which individuals are able to follow their own values and self-directed life course within their particular social context, while being emotionally present with others, rather than living reactively by the cues of those close to them. They do not spend their life energy on winning approval, attacking others, intellectualizing, keeping themselves emotionally walled off, or maneuvering in relationships to obtain control or emotional comfort. They can move freely from emotional closeness in person-to-person relationships to work on their personal life goals. They can calmly state their beliefs or feelings (or, when appropriate, refrain from stating their feelings or beliefs)— without having to attack others or defend themselves. In their personal relationships they can relate warmly and openly without needing to focus on others or on activities or impersonal things in order to find common ground.

How would you characterize your presence in relationships? Can you express compassion and empathy while being able to voice your own opinions? Do you prefer to maintain a certain distance? Are approval and acceptance important to you? Do your defenses easily kick in?

Take stock of the degree to which you are comfortable in your own skin. Can you honestly say that you move through the world with a clear sense of self, relating openly and maturely to those around you?

Think about someone to whom you are close and any of the ways in which that relationship could be improved.

Understanding how we behave in relationships can often point us to larger life issues worth working on.

Gratitude

R EALIZE THAT THE world is not perfect but you can be grateful no matter what condition you are in. For example,

- You can be grateful whether you are sick or healthy. If you are sick, you may choose to be grateful for the times that you feel good. If you are not sick, you can be grateful for your good health.

- You can be grateful in difficult situations. In such instances gratitude may not solve your problem, but it can help you find positives even when they may not be apparent. If you have been in an accident, you can be grateful that you survived it. You can also be grateful for the things that you have left versus those things that you have lost.

- You can be grateful in the presence of loss. For example, the death of a loved one is a profoundly sorrowful event. However, statements like "I am grateful for the time we had together" or "He/she lived a long and healthy life" can negate emotions such as anger, sorrow, blame, guilt, and shame.

Are you able to express gratitude even in the face of challenges? Take a moment to reflect on a recent difficult time and the ways in which you did—or could—express gratitude despite the difficulties. Make a vow to try to do this the next time a difficult situation presents itself.

It may be useful to create a short list. For every difficult or challenging situation on your list, think of five positive aspects of that situation for which you are grateful.

Practicing gratitude in this way can be contagious—once you start, it will become a habit.

Goals

O N THE SURFACE, flexibility, or willingness and ability to change, appears to be almost the polar opposite of determination. But the two do not actually contradict each other at all. Being determined has to do with the strength of an intention, not rigidity in holding it. Flexibility, in turn, speaks of being able to accept changes on the road of relationship, and the ability to move off the dime in order to reach a goal.

Recall a recent disagreement with a friend or loved one in which you could have been more flexible. What might you have said or done differently to show the strength of your intention and feeling, and yet your ability to accept this person's point of view? Do you see how flexibility and strength of intention can be part of the same response?

Change

I T IS REMARKABLE how little we know about experience that is happening right now. . . . The present moment can be held hostage by either the past or the future. The past can eclipse the present by casting so strong a shadow on it that the present can only confirm what was already known and can add little more. . . . The future can also annihilate the present by reorganizing it so much and so fast that the present becomes ephemeral and almost passes out of existence.

The challenge is to imagine the present moment in some kind of dialogic equilibrium with the past and future. If the present moment is not well anchored in a past and future it floats off as a meaningless speck. If it is too well anchored it becomes diminished.

Try—right now—to think about the "right now." Do not think about the past; do not think about the present. Realize how much effort it takes to remain in the here and now. During the course of your day today, bring yourself back to the here and now as much as possible. Notice the difference this intentional approach makes in your experience of the day.

Health

HEALTH IS DEFINED by the intelligence of life—that innate drive in biological organisms to self-correct, and self-balance. This is wholeness. As a concept, wholeness is so simple and ubiquitous that everyone simply overlooks it. Yet, in the same way, it is so complex and nuanced that scientists often fail to perceive it. Nevertheless, wholeness guides health by acknowledging the innate intelligence of life. Without wholeness life becomes disorder and disease; with it life can achieve bodily, mental, and spiritual health. When it is lost, anxiety, depression, disease, and chronic pain emerge. When it is found, inner peace, true joy, and physical healing return.

What does health mean to you? Do you experience a wholeness when you think of health? What can you do to feel more whole in your life? When we feel sad, lonely, or troubled over some problem in our life, we tend to fixate on it until it becomes difficult to see beyond it. Your body naturally strives to be in balance, and sometimes the solution to feeling "off" is as simple as looking beyond the problem itself and paying attention to other facets of your life.

The next time you find yourself in a rut, make a lunch date with an old friend, stroll through a park and admire the trees, eat a healthy meal in place of your Friday night pizza tradition, watch one less TV show or movie a week, or pick up a book you've been wanting to read. Make a conscious effort to bring a sense of wholeness to your life.

Forgiveness

THERE IS A time to search for the past, even to be immersed in it. But there is also a time to let go. This is true of life-transforming events as well as of more trivial ones.

Letting go does not mean uncontrollable forgetting, but rather a shifting of perspectives. More and more, attention is turned toward the here and now or to prospective visions of the future. Once the past recalled has been integrated into the fabric of one's life, attention can focus on it as needed.

Just as the decision to take up the search or to confront any particular memory is a matter of individual readiness, so is the decision to move on; only the self can decide when the time has come to let go. This decision often evolves in a natural, almost imperceptible way as a consequence of integrative processes that, however deliberate, have an unconscious dimension. Becoming more comfortable with who one was and is makes it possible to relax and shift focus. Learning that the past will always be there and that the self is safe from getting lost makes it possible to explore new territory.

How comfortable are you with events in your past? Are you able to carry the past with you in a way that is comfortable and nurturing without being suffocating?

Try this today: tell yourself, "My memories form an abundant and unfamiliar landscape that I am excited to explore." Remember this when thinking of the past, both the pleasant and unpleasant parts of it.

Mindfulness

A FELT SENSE IS a fresh, immediate, here-and-now experience that is actually the organism forming its next step in the situation the person is living in. Felt senses form because we deliberately invite them to form. We say, with genuine curiosity, "How am I right now?"—and wait for the answer. We wonder inwardly, "What is it about this that bothers me so much?" and wait to feel what comes.

The pause, the inner intention of asking, enables a felt sense to form. Of course it is not necessary to have all this conceptual apparatus for felt sensing to happen, since anyone can have a felt sense without knowing the term. When a felt sense forms there is always some kind of pausing, some kind of turning toward "something." What we then find may be murky, unclear, vague, and not feel like much—but the fact that it formed is already the beginning of our life moving forward in new and fresh ways.

Try to feel yourself sensing today without judgment and without fear. Take time during various moments of the day to ask yourself, with intention, "How am I right now?" Does a finer attention to your everyday experiences open up new avenues of action? Do you find yourself moving through the day with an increased sense of purpose?

Try to incorporate this basic mindfulness practice into your life and notice the profound impact it can have.

Stress

MAINTAINING A "SENSE of good humor" speaks of "being funny," but the key to this good humor is in not turning the "funniness" on another person as a distraction or attack. A sense of good humor refers to recognizing humor in oneself, or in the things one has done or failed to do, or things another has done or failed to do, and then relating that to life or to others in such a way that kindness, not acerbity, prevails. One especially valuable aspect of a sense of good humor is demonstrated at times of stress; it can be very helpful in reducing conflicts and reestablishing equilibrium.

Try to notice how you wield your sense of humor. Does it tend to defuse tense situations, or create them? Can you make any changes in your use of humor that will enliven situations rather than enflame them?

The next time you face a stressful situation, ask yourself whether a well-timed and appropriate dollop of humor might help.

Family

A PART OF US always longs to go back to the family—but to have it be different. This time, you tell yourself, you'll hold onto your adult perspective and not become defensive. You won't get caught up in your parents' battles or compete with your siblings for attention. Maturity, objectivity, humor, and serenity will carry the day, if only you can keep your distance.

Sometimes you can even manage to hold onto your sense of self for a little while. But then something seemingly trivial happens—perhaps your father makes a sarcastic joke at your mother's expense and she goes silent. This little scene may have occurred a hundred times in the past. In a second you fall into the role you played in childhood, jabbing back, moving in to protect your mother. In your frustration you gossip with your siblings about how impossible your parents are and you wonder how you managed to survive all the underlying hostility in your family for so long.

If you want to reconnect with your family, you will need to develop a kind of empathy, recognizing that you and your family belong to each other. This requires an acceptance of the almost mystical fundamental human connectedness we have as people. It means accepting that whatever terrible things another person might do, that person is human and we could be in his or her shoes. It means accepting parents with all their imperfections, which is not the same as accepting their imperfections themselves.

Think about what your experiences are when you spend time with your family of origin. Bearing in mind what you've just read, what can you do in the future to foster a sense of connection with your family? How can you accept family members for who they are? What will you gain for yourself in doing so?

Communication

SILENCE IS GOLDEN. Listening includes silence and it also requires active investment in what the other person is saying and who the other person is. Listening is a gift. Listening does not require agreement. Listening requires respect.

Make a concerted effort today to choose a moment during a difficult conversation to listen with intention. Stifle any urge you might have to jump in and fill the silences. Instead, listen longer, and think more deeply, about what is being said. Notice how this act of listening with intention impacts how, and what, you hear.

Self-Awareness

OWEVER WE DEFINE it, men and women generally benefit from hearing and heeding their voices. People who tune themselves out end up stuck in bad jobs and unhappy marriages, and live by crazy rules from their families of origin. People who listen to themselves change careers, evolve in good marriages or leave painful marriages, and challenge their aging parents, all because they know that things are not the way they should be.

So hearing your voice can be as simple as attending to yourself for a few minutes or as difficult as struggling through months of therapy. In some ways it's the same as self-acceptance.

Take notice of your own inner voice today. Is it telling you things you've been tuning out in favor of received ideas and outside authority? How can you attune yourself to a true inner voice?

Problem Solving

Setbacks are part of the path to success. I think about it—when babies learn to walk, there are *many* falls on the way to success. We don't expect perfection on the first try from a baby, and we shouldn't expect it from ourselves, either. Sometimes those "falls" can be quite helpful—they can show us what we may need to change about our plans. The only way they spell failure is if we decide to quit because these slips have happened.

Does your past look any different if you remove from it the concept of failure? Does anything that seemed like a failure at the time reveal itself as a slipup from which you've already learned something? Recall a story from your past in which you have done something "wrong" or made a mistake. Is there a way to reframe that story by focusing less on the mistakes made and more on the lessons learned?

Relationships

Human beings have two basic jobs: to be individuals and to connect with others. Within the couple and family, healthy individuals are able to balance these two jobs in a way that works well for both the individual and the couple or family. The healthy person has the ability to know how to be close without losing a sense of self and how to be apart without becoming disconnected.

Think of times in your recent past when you have felt that you compromised your sense of self for your partner. Think about what you could have done differently; remember the resentments that may have arisen because of this. Promise yourself: Today I will try to become close with my partner without compromising my sense of self.

Change

MANY PEOPLE BELIEVE that a person changes from the inside out, that is, some sort of internal changes occur in thoughts and feelings and then behavioral changes will follow. It may be true. At the same time, it also may be true that outward changes can create internal changes. As they say, you can "fake it until you make it." Sometimes action comes first, and then insight or understanding follows.

Are you acting to create the life you want to have. What little things can you do differently to get into the habit of living well? Can you think of one or two little changes to make—today—that will help you just one small step closer to the life you want to be leading tomorrow?

Forgiveness

SOMETIMES UNHAPPINESS IN our present life is due to the distorted past we have created in our memory. In such cases, the only way to become content in the present is to force ourselves to remember the past more accurately. For life to guide us, we should remember our history in as unbiased, unprejudiced, dispassionate a manner as possible. It is best to choose our past carefully.

Recall a difficult memory from your past. It doesn't have to be your worst memory—just a less-than-pleasant one. Is there a way to think more objectively about what happened, perhaps giving yourself a break for behavior you may now regret? In doing so, see that your past mistakes and painful experiences need not define your present or future life.

Goals

ULTIMATELY THE GREATEST payoff for human behavior may not be external rewards or punishment, not money, or pleasure, or avoidance of pain, or even the promised reward of a better life hereafter. The real payoff may be pouring all our being into reaching a goal, whether it be winning a race or saving another's life. The goal is irrelevant; it's the striving that counts.

Bring to mind a current or recent struggle. Can you find any satisfaction in your drive to overcome this challenge, whether or not you can (or did)?

Stress

I T IS IMPORTANT for you to connect to the part of your mind that can choose what you wish to focus on at any given time, just like you already have prescribed times to do other things such as wake up, go to work, eat lunch, though it may vary from day to day. In the same way that you've developed the habit of doing those things at those times you can create a prescribed time to worry or obsess. Then you can have the freedom to enjoy your day knowing that you have created a space in time to focus on the accumulated (insert what applies, such as worries, fears, resentment, grief, or obsessive thoughts). You can even make notes for that later "worry" time so that you can let go of the thoughts and worries now, secure in the fact that you will get back to them later.

⬭ *You may wish to set aside 15 minutes of the day as your "worry time." Make a promise to yourself: Today I choose to enjoy my day; I will try to defer the worrisome thoughts that come to me to a time of my choosing.*

Family

A PARENT WHO IS a leader has accepted the absolute fact that families work better when parents are in charge. The leader realizes that adults have to make rules and that it is up to children to follow those rules. The parents stay in charge by developing a combination of negotiable and nonnegotiable rules. It is up to the parent to decide which rules are negotiable and which are not. When the rules are not negotiable, the adult stays in charge by making very specific rules, choosing and consistently enforcing rewards and consequences, including children in the process when appropriate, telling children what the rules are, and checking for understanding.

How clear are the rules in your household? Is there one in particular you could clarify today? Are you comfortable giving your children some agency in helping to create rules? What will be gained by empowering your children in this way?

Communication

E VERY INTERACTION IS a two-way street. In every conversation or exchange between two (or more) people, there's
a lot of mutual influence going on whether you're aware of it or
not. Usually, we're not. In learning to become more open and
connected to others, it's crucial that we develop deep understanding of the mutuality of relating.

*Become a close observer of your interactions with
others today. Can you notice the influence (even if small)
that others have on you (and you on them)? What is
happening in terms of your emotions and actions when
interactions are going particularly well or particularly
badly?*

Self-Awareness

I F ONE CAN make deeper and better connections with one-self, others, and some bigger sense of things or meanings after a crisis, one can thrive or grow as a result of the crisis.

Think of a recent or past event in your life that you consider to have been a crisis. How did you mature as a result of it? How were you changed for the good? Remember this, and be proud of yourself for how you responded.

Relationships

W HEN MOST PEOPLE are asked to describe their ideal partner or child or friend, the word "yet" often sneaks into the description. We want someone who can be spontaneous yet responsible, sensitive yet assertive, a good talker yet a good listener, too. From the perspective of temperament, these "yets" are usually splitting off the positive aspects of a temperamental trait while attempting to leave behind the negative components. Such a profile can be extremely difficult to find in the real world (present company excluded, of course). High levels of sociability, for example, may be a wonderful trait in a friend but not uncommonly can be associated with a certain degree of dependence or even "neediness." Yet changing a more negative dimension runs the risk that the associated positive features will be diminished as well. Ironically, the end result could well be a person with very average levels of temperament dimensions that may strike many as being somewhat "vanilla."

⌒⌒ *Bring to mind three close friends or family members and draw a basic table, with their names listed vertically in columns. Next, create three rows across the page: one for Positive Traits, one for Negative Traits, and one for Overall Character—a single adjective that immediately comes to mind when you are asked to characterize the person. Fill in the empty fields in the table for each friend or loved one until it's complete. Now consider how your feelings about someone would change if that perceived negative trait weren't there. How would that person be different? Would you feel as close to him or her? How would your relationship to the person change?*

Change

I N LIFE, MANY things are beyond our control. But we have some freedom. We can choose how we eat and we can choose what to focus our attention on and how we make sense of the world. By exercising those freedoms, we can create change in our lives.

Tell yourself: *I make dozens of decisions a day— some big and some little. Today I will practice making each decision thoughtfully and with intention. I will do my best not to sleepwalk through the day. At the end of the day I will notice how different it felt to live each moment with meaning and purpose.*

Health

E ATING HEALTHY FOOD is an important part of wellness.
Choosing healthy food instead of junk food can help your
brain work better, help keep your mood stable, and keep up
your energy level. It is easy to grab a hamburger and an order
of fries instead of a bowl of soup and a salad. A hamburger,
with its high fat contact, might taste better, is easier to eat
"on the run," and may even be less expensive. A bag of potato
chips may be more appealing than a piece of fruit. The people
who sell us fast food understand how to get us to eat what
they want to sell, instead of what is good for us. Unfortunately,
high-fat, high-sugar food will usually cause us to feel less ener-
getic or "sharp." Choose food wisely. Pick brain food instead
of junk food.

Do an honest assessment of the foods you are
eating today. Are you choosing the healthiest options?
Try keeping a food journal for just a week. At the

end of the week, assess the healthiness of your food consumption. If you are not happy with the results, make a promise to yourself to make a few small changes each week until your overall food intake is healthier.

Forgiveness

THE SEARCH FOR the past is in many instances a private endeavor. Whether it involves a trip to an old hometown, the unpacking of a trunk, reading an old journal, or attempting to write an autobiography, the quest confronts the self with the complexities and mysteries of memory. How strange the difference between what one remembered and what one now discovers! How remarkable the accuracy of a particular recollection! How curious the loss of a significant detail or episode! The discovery of transformations and discontinuities can be disquieting as well as difficult to comprehend. And disputes that arise between self-now and self-then can be as contentious, even painful, as disputes between self and other.

If you can, go to an old box or trunk or storage unit and dig up some concrete things from your past. Think about how these items stimulate your memories of an incident or person. Do the memories spurred by them match what you remembered before?

Goals

*D*estiny IS THE pattern of limits and talents that constitutes the "givens" in life. It is in the confronting of these limits that our creativity emerges. Our destiny cannot be canceled out; we cannot erase it or substitute anything else for it. But we can choose how we shall respond, how we shall live out our talents which confront us.

Think about some impediments that you create for yourself in realizing some of your own goals. Can you commit, for today, at least, to confronting just one of these obstacles and changing it?

Family

WHEN PARENTS ENCOURAGE their children, they praise efforts and identify any successes or partial successes. They identify specific things that please them about their children and communicate that clearly to them. Children are encouraged to speak up about their goals, hopes, and dreams about the future. Children are encouraged to talk about what matters to them. Parents listen, even when it hurts—and it will. When parents take the risk to encourage children to talk, children will say things that run counter to the parents' values and goals. When we listen, we need to keep our thoughts to ourselves. Remember, listening does not equal agreement.

How have your conversations with your children tended to go recently? Why might they not be opening up to you as much as you would like?

Today, make a conscious effort to approach your children in a nonjudgmental manner, listening to their hopes and thoughts and restraining yourself from giving advice. Notice how your children may begin to open up if you practice this sort of conversation on a regular basis.

Communication

I T IS A misconception that communication ought to be the norm in relationships. What may matter most is the ability of couples to repair things when they go wrong.

⟨☉⟩ *Be honest with yourself: The last time you had a disagreement with your partner, were you more interested in proving your point or in moving beyond the argument to a place of repair? Spend today thinking of ways in which you and your partner are successful at patching things up, and promise yourself to draw on those skills the next time you have a difference of opinion.*

Self-Awareness

THE EFFORT TO expand one's narrative voice is what makes us human, building the solidarity that connects each of us to a community, making us larger than ourselves, working across differences for the sum of our alliances. Being human is an endless effort to collect our distributed selves from all the locations where they are scattered, forging them into a more coherent account of who we are.

Take some time to make a list of the various identities you have in the world—at work, at home, in the various communities of which you are a part. Realize that you may be carrying more identities with you than you realize. Think about ways in which you are successful in integrating them and ways in which you might improve that assimilation. Can you draw from your strengths in one area of your life and apply them to other areas?

Problem Solving

E VEN IF YOUR parents, teachers, fellow students, or others around you often talked negatively to you as you were growing up, you can learn how to talk to yourself in a more useful way. Besides making you feel better, this can support you in your activities, relationships, and goals in life.

For example, try saying the sentence, "What else can I enjoy right now?" to yourself, and notice how it changes what you attend to, and how you feel in response.

That sentence directs your attention toward what you can enjoy in the present moment, rather than the complaints and problems that so often occupy our attention and make us feel bad. Even in the worst situation there is always something to enjoy, so this instruction never contradicts your reality. And it also doesn't contradict any grumpy voice that is complaining about all the nasty stuff. It doesn't oppose it by saying "but"; it just directs your attention to other aspects of your experience, saying "and," joining what a critical voice might be attending to with noticing what you can enjoy. If you say that sentence repeatedly until it becomes an unconscious mantra, it can reorient your life in a way that is both useful and enjoyable.

At some point during the day today when you are bored or stressed or uncomfortable, try asking yourself if there is something else that you could be enjoying at the moment. Even if you can't change what you are doing, is there a way to enjoy at least part of it?

Communication

POSITIVE COMMENTS ARE the major means for establishing a good relationship. Imagine a salt shaker filled not with salt but with all the ways to say "yes!" (things like: "good point"; "I see"; "yes"; "that makes sense, tell me more"; "you're starting to convince me"; "I never thought of it that way"; "if that's so important to you let's find a way to make that happen"; "say more about how you feel and what you need"; and so on). Use that salt shaker throughout your interactions, and you'll instantly become a "master."

Conversely, imagine a salt shaker filled not with salt but with all the ways to say "no!" (things like: "that's ridiculous!"; "no"; "that is so stupid"; "you're stupid"; "you're making no sense"; "be logical!"; "shut up!"; "stop talking"; "you're an idiot"; "you're a jerk"; "how can you be so insensitive?"; "you never have cared about me"; "you're so selfish"; and so on). Use that salt shaker throughout your interactions and you'll instantly become a "disaster."

Of course, we all use the second salt shaker some of the time. But the disasters do it much more often. With the masters, there is far more positive emotion, warmth, affection, being there for each other, interest, humor, understanding, and empathy. Masters say "yes" in the various ways more often than they say "no" through anger, hostility, insult, disgust, contempt, sarcasm, sadness, disappointment, belittling, disagreement, and emotional withdrawal.

During the day today, make a conscious effort to reach for the "yes" salt shaker before the "no" shaker. Notice what a difference this strategy makes in your daily interactions. Notice how you feel better, not only about others but about yourself. Being able to put a positive spin on things feels good.

Gratitude

GRATITUDE IS A very accessible positive aging strategy since it primarily involves shifting your state of mind from one valence (negative) to another (positive). It does take practice and repetition in order for it to become a natural reaction to a negative life challenge. What is powerful about gratitude is that you don't even need to engage in any physical behavior or even lift a finger to generate feelings of gratitude. You can do it all in your head.

To demonstrate this, sit back in your chair for a moment. Close your eyes. Recollect the best thing that happened to you during the past week. Take a minute and pay attention to those feelings that were associated with this positive event. Are you grateful for the event? Assuming that you are, you can dwell on the reasons that you feel grateful. As you practice this simple exercise for just a few minutes, you will notice that your affect will change in a positive direction and not just about the event, but for other things as well. You may feel that "It's great to be alive" or "Good things happen to me."

Gratitude is a state of mind, and today I will practice it. At the end of today, promise yourself that you will take some quiet time to reflect upon a few things for which you are grateful. Try to feel gratitude for one or two specific events that happened today, as well as a few ongoing events or relationships in your life.

Goals

IT MAY ACTUALLY be difficult to think about your goals. It might be hard to allow yourself to want anything, especially if you have been disappointed over and over. Even if you have goals, it might be hard to go from big, general goals like "I want my life to be better" to more specific goals that you can actually work on.

The more specific and concrete your goals are, the more likely you are to actually reach them. Goals can be separated into short-term ones and long-term ones. Short-term goals are things you can work toward over the next few months. Long-term goals may take years. Dreams are also important. Goals may be difficult but they are also possible. Dreams may not be possible, but we still think about and hope for them. Getting a part-time job may be a short-term goal—something that may be difficult but is possible to accomplish over the next couple of months. Finishing school may be a long-term goal; it may take years of work. Becoming an astronaut may be a dream. It is unlikely that any adult could become an astronaut if they had a significant gap in school or work or had a serious illness. Even if it is unrealistic, it is good to have dreams. Dreams help to keep hope alive, and there is always the hope that a dream can come true.

Take a minute to reflect on your long-term goals. What simple things can you do today or this week to help you reach those goals?

Take another moment to think about your hopes and dreams. Striving for a goal, even if it is unattainable, can be reinvigorating.

Change

SOMETIMES, PARADOXICAL AS it may seem, acceptance is the best approach to change. If you have done all you can do to make change or you find that struggling to change something creates more problems, the best path might be surrender and acceptance. Sometimes the acceptance leads to a breakthrough in being able to change. At other times, just accepting creates a sense of peace, which dissolves the problematic sense of things.

Are there difficulties in your life that you feel all right about accepting over the long term? Does your honest appraisal of your limitations open up some new possibility that you hadn't foreseen?

Self-Awareness

WHENEVER WE LOOK at what is alive, whether we are looking at a tree out the window or a laughing child running across the yard, we see life process moving forward. There is a natural process for moving from potential to actualization. What happens now was, a moment before, ready to happen, in potential. Yet what happens is not determined. There are possibilities, and while those possibilities are specific to that person, in that life situation, in that context, within that specificity, there is enormous creative potential.

Consider the act of walking or running. When you are walking, and even more when you are running, your body leans into your next step. This is a metaphor for the process of life itself—we are always "leaning into" our next steps. When we inhale, our bodies are getting ready to exhale. The process of inhaling implies forward to exhaling. And of course the process of exhaling implies forward to inhaling.

What if we try to stop that process—what happens? As an experiment, try exhaling and then holding your breath

rather than inhaling. The result is a feeling of discomfort—
becoming stronger and stronger as time goes on. (Okay, you
can inhale now!)

*Try to take notice of the cycle of implying forward
during the day today. While you recognize how each
moment "leans in" to the next, are these ways you can
learn to savor each moment on its own? In this continual
process of potential turning into actualization, is there a
point at which you can feel inspired creatively?*

Mindfulness

HUMAN LIFE IS of a piece. We can't "get it together"; it *is* together. We divide it—distinguishing material reality from psychic reality, relationships from drives, psychology from physiology, and conscious from unconscious. We divide the intrapsychic and intersubjective, internal reality from external reality, the spiritual from the psychological, self from other, and personal life from cultural life. Such distinctions, however important, cannot capture the rich interwoven fabric of our humanity. Spiritual and emotional experience and growth evolve in concert, and, when functioning harmoniously, their interplay is seamless.

Take time today to think about the ways in which your life may be divided or not cohesive. Can you envision any ways in which you might unify aspects of your life that are disparate? How would doing so increase the overall quality of your life?

Stress

ONE CAN'T BEGIN to address the topic of healing trauma without dealing with the fact that trauma is an aberration of memory. It freezes us in a past event that thereafter dictates our entire perception of reality. The past event is ever-present, awaiting its chance to intrude on our daily life based on the subtlest of cues.

Locked in the crucible of terror created by the traumatic experience, we dance like a puppet on strings controlled by a manic and repetitive puppeteer. Our thoughts, our choices, our values, our behavior, even the control of our bodies seem to be governed not by conscious intent but by some inner tyrant that operates with an unknown and sinister agenda. The messages provided by our very thoughts are alien, nonsensical, and divorced from the events around us and from our moment-to-moment perceptions.

Our storehouse of old memories on which we base the perception of our identity is fragmented, distorted, at times terrifying, at times confusing. We respond to events in our daily life with emotions that seem to arise spontaneously with a degree of intensity that alone is terrifying. Deep in our hearts we recognize that our inner life makes no sense, and overlying it all is a deep sense of shame. Seeking safety, we find ourselves shrinking into a smaller and smaller space until there is no space at all around us that we can call ours. And still the world seems able to assault us with messages that somehow instill fear.

If you have suffered a trauma in your life, take a moment to think about it now. How has this trauma caused you to shrink in your present life? Can you do anything to fight back and expand into the safety that is now?

Family

WHEN CHILDREN SENSE that other people in their family want to know them—*really* know them—and also sense that, although there might be initial disappointment and conflict, they will be valued even if they are different, they are more likely to reveal themselves.

How might you encourage your children or other family members to fully reveal their inner worlds to you? Is there anything you're afraid of hearing? Are you sending out subtle signals to your children not to reveal their true selves to you? If so, what work can you do with yourself to stop doing this, and to be more open?

Relationships

I T IS SAID that love is a decision that we make every day. We demonstrate that love in word and action. Staying connected, likewise, is a choice to spend time and to interact with one another. Healthy connection allows individuals to be close and also to move apart from one another as each engages in separate activities. When couples return from their separate activities, they have more to share with each other due to their unique experiences.

Are you comfortable with the amount of together and away time you spend with your partner? Tell yourself: Today I will be a better partner by cultivating my own passions and interests.

Change

ONE OF THE ways to think about change is to consider problems not as fixed entities—things—but rather as patterns. This view can help foster change by thinking of problems less as set and unchangeable burdens and more as processes. Patterns can be changed at any point in the process. *Things* are much harder to change.

Try to deduce the pattern in a problem that arises today and see what a difference it makes in terms of how you approach managing the problem. How does thinking about a problem as a pattern rather than as a thing change your ability to grapple with it?

Forgiveness

WE OFTEN ARE told to let sleeping dogs lie or that the past is past. My response to the first is, Sleeping dogs may well awaken at the most inopportune moments. Better to wake the dog when you're in a position to care for it and tame it. And to the second I would say, If the past were to stay in the past we would not have to take notice of it. But the past constantly influences the meaning that we give to the present. It would be better for the present to influence the meaning that we give to the past.

Yes, the past is still alive in the present, and because of this, it can be influenced, modified, deepened, and given new meanings. We cannot change the events of the past, but we can change the meanings we give to them. By changing the meanings, we can alter the influence of those past events on the present. In the process of effecting such changes, we often find that we can make new sense of the past in ways that are liberating—ways that carry hope for our current relationships, as well as those that lie in the future.

Think about an event from your past and the ways in which that event may still intrude into the present. Can you make one small change in how you think about this event? If you do that, what do you notice about how you experience thoughts of the past? Does that change impact how you think about the present?

Mindfulness

ACHIEVING BALANCE MAY not be as easy today with the outrageous demands we place on ourselves and our children to do something with every moment. However, if you ask yourself about each activity, "Is this activity in service of my purpose in life?" it can help you decide whether to do it or not.

Today, consider the activities and obligations you've set up for yourself. What do you get out of each one, and how does it fit into your larger goals for yourself?

Forgiveness

P ERHAPS THE MOST interesting thing we may gain in the
process of transformation from trauma is insight not only
into the meaning of previously distressing and even disabling
symptoms, but also into other personal features we have
always assumed we inherited from our parents. Recognizing
these traits for what they are allows us to view ourselves not
only with empathy and understanding but also with a little
humor. Perhaps the ability to laugh at ourselves with wisdom
and without regret is the ultimate gift of healing from trauma.

 Think about how you treat yourself. Are you too
hard on yourself? Are you able to give yourself a break
from time to time? Just for today, commit to going easy
on yourself and have compassion for the ways in which
you behave.

Family

TRANSFORMING FAMILIES IS about helping them be open to receiving the gifts that their unique children bring. These are gifts they never expected, talents they do not share, and interests that seem to come from nowhere. When we are open to our children and we are brave enough to see them, we are transformed.

Think about your children or other ones. Are you truly open to who they are, even the parts of them that you wish were different? In what ways could you be more receptive to meeting them on their own terms? Commit to focusing on this issue today and notice the difference in your experience of them.

Communication

IT BECOMES EASY to sound as though you are making accusations against someone when you are both upset. "You really made me angry"; "You were so inconsiderate." Statements tend to want to escape our lips starting with "You, you, you!" This is a simple shift, but resolving *not* to begin sentences with *you*, and instead starting with *I*, can soften your statements and take out the sting. Better still, following up with the word *feel* can really help you express yourself without blaming the other person for your experience. This moves the point of the conversation from accusations, which can automatically bring out defensiveness in the other person, to an explanation of your personal experience, which is more likely to invite understanding.

Taking things a step further, the following structure can make things even more clear, while keeping communication from becoming combative: "When you [whatever behavior you observed], I feel [whatever emotions you are feeling]." This lets the person know exactly what it was that upset you and exactly how you felt as a result. This helps you avoid other communication pitfalls such as interpreting the person's motives and applying negative labels and allows you to focus simply on the behavior and the feelings, which lets a more emotionally neutral discussion ensue.

Try incorporating "I" statements the next time you're expressing hurt or disappointment to your partner or a friend and see if he or she reacts with more understanding than usual. Try saying "I feel _____ when you _____."

Self-Awareness

R EAL COURAGE OFTEN happens in quiet moments with no
fanfare; sometimes it's in the simple decision to take one
step and one day at a time.

    *Try making a list of the large and small acts of
courage you engage in daily. Post the list in your home to
remind yourself of your own daily heroisms.*

Problem Solving

IF YOU WALK out to the parking lot and find that your car has a flat tire, don't get caught up in your annoyance; don't start telling yourself a story about how life is unfair. Change the tire. Once you do, the problem will be solved, and you can feel good about your accomplishment. Proactivity is the key. If we are able to do what we need to do in spite of how we feel, if we focus on our sense of purpose, we create a constructive life, and this, in turn, allows us to feel better about ourselves.

Think about the last time you were annoyed about something or encountered some obstacle or small problem in your life. In looking back at that situation, can you think of any ways in which you could have approached that situation differently—with an eye toward solving the problem rather than wallowing in it? How can you use this solution-focused attitude in the days and weeks to come?

Relationships

WHILE WE CAN'T change other people, we can alter how we behave in our relationships, and often that's enough to make a profound difference in the entire dynamic. Changing our part in the "dance"—the interplay of expected roles and reactions—creates room for new ways of being with each other.

Boundary setting, however, can also foster closeness. It's not all about pushing people away. When we set boundaries with others, we actually allow them to become closer to us than we may have otherwise allowed, because we know that there is a line—that they can get close to us without going too far. Without healthy boundaries, people tend to either let others get too close, and then push them way back, or cut people off entirely. (Ironically, a cut-off relationship is not considered one with healthy boundaries, because there is no closeness to begin with; boundaries suggest that people can get close, but not too close, not that they cannot get close at all.)

Think about the relationships in your life. What constitutes healthy boundaries? Choose one relationship to focus on and imagine how you might reset its boundaries. Do you need to create more distance, or more closeness?

Change

W HEN WINTER COMES and the temperature begins to
fall, rooms must be heated and one must wear warm
clothing outside in order to remain comfortable. If the temperature falls even lower, more heat and warm clothing are
needed. In other words, change becomes necessary to rees-
tablish the norm, both for comfort and survival. The desired
change is achieved through applying the opposite of what pro-
duced the deviance (e.g., heat vs. cold).

*Tell yourself: Today I will think of some things
in my life that have changed recently and notice how I
have been able to adapt to them and maintain my sense
of calm and equilibrium. I will think about whether the
strategies I have already used in the past can be applied
to changes I might encounter in the future.*

Health

THIS TEMPLE THAT is your body, which blends so complexly with your mind and feelings, is your best friend, even if your relationship with it is conflicted. Because you need your body in order to live, it matters a great deal whether you listen to—and take care of—its needs. It also matters that you are aware of the quality of your thoughts and feelings as they move through, and live in, your body.

Becoming more grounded, more whole as a bodymind, requires taking time to commune with your body. Your sense of wholeness is enhanced if you take some time each day, or once a week, to talk to your body and listen to what it has to convey to you. Just *residing in* your body isn't enough. The quality of your relationship with this miracle that gives you physical life is a powerful element in creating a sense of either psychological wholeness or alienation.

Do you listen to what your body needs? You might take some time today to sit quietly, hands resting in your lap, and simply take note of how your body feels and what it's telling you. Is there a certain tightness or soreness somewhere that you hadn't taken notice of before? Do you feel your heart beat slowing, relaxing? What are you being told to pay attention to?

Take a moment to ask your body what it needs; it often knows better than the mind does.

Communication

RATHER THAN BEING consumed by worries about the future or preoccupations with the past, living fully in the present is an art form that liberates the mind to relieve mental suffering. These are the ways we develop presence in our own lives. Being present can also be seen as the most important element of helping others heal.

We are filled with potential. Health in many ways can be seen as bathing in a wide-open pool of possibility. Unhealth can be viewed as various rigid and chaotic ways we become unable to be present with this broad freedom. Without ways to strengthen the mind—to build the resilience that comes with being present, with being mindful—we are at risk of becoming overwhelmed in the moment, and of burning out in the long run.

How we bring a full and receptive self into engagement with others, how we are present in life, can help in everything we do including the challenging pursuit of helping others and preserving and improving our physical world.

⌒⌒ *This is a hard one, but try: Promise yourself today that you will live only in the present moment, focusing only on what is actually happening, not what just happened or what might happen later in the day. Notice how you experience the day differently.*

Mindfulness

LIFE IS A basically messy business. Everyday living is organic and unpredictable, no matter how much we may try to nail it down and get all our "ducks in a row." Within this ever-changing context of never knowing what will happen next, it is all too easy to get caught up in the hassles of daily life, to focus on the many things that *don't* go as expected, on moments that are difficult or irritating.

When you begin to live more mindfully, it becomes increasingly likely that you will notice how many things go *right* during any given day. These supportive, easy, or satisfying moments come in all shapes and sizes. On the simplest level, you might take the time to notice that you wanted cereal for breakfast and there was just enough milk left in the refrigerator to make that possible.

On a more dramatic level, the accident you were certain was about to happen didn't; the illness you feared was serious turns out to be nothing more than a twenty-four-hour bug; the person you had dinner with last week seems to be interested in a deeper relationship—just when you'd given up thinking anyone new would come into your life.

Try to embrace the moments of uncertainty in your day. You might find that things go your way more often than you typically notice.

Mindfulness

WITH FOCUSED ATTENTION and clear awareness, typical ways of experiencing through the rational mind are bypassed to discover a deeper nature. We are all born with an enlightened mind. We just don't know how to access it. Meditation shows the way.

Examine your beliefs about your ability to change your life. Think about the ways in which a commitment to thought could result in a commitment to change. Being truly open to change is the first essential step in allowing change to be possible. Do you believe you can change? Really believe it?

Today, promise yourself that you will focus on your ability to change, and believe it.

Self-Awareness

MOST SIMPLY PUT, our ego is our thinking mind. The word "ego" comes from Latin, meaning "I." Our ego is the part of us concerned with personal identity ("I am a therapist"), achievements ("I earn straight A's"), possessions ("My house"), and even our emotions ("I am angry"). All these statements say something about our identity, but they don't really describe who we are underneath all that. If you took away your job or your house, or your grades, you would still be you! Since your ego is what you think of as your personal identity, it is what separates you from others. Your ego compares, judges, and criticizes: "I am ugly," "She is thinner," "I am fat." When you criticize others or feel criticized, know that it is your ego at work. However, you do not need to think of your ego as bad or unimportant. Your ego is necessary. You need an ego to live on this planet and effectively interact in the world, to think, plan, prepare, and provide. It might help to think of your ego as the "human" part of human being. The problem arises when you think your ego is all that you are, and you have no connection to your soul self.

Your soul, on the other hand, is the "being" part of human being. Your soul self is the part of you separate from your thoughts and emotions. Rather than "I am this" or "I am that" your soul self is simply expressed in the phrase "I am." To define the soul exactly is impossible because it is not a thing, it is your *essence*—in other words, you don't have a soul, you *are* a soul. Your soul self is your essence, but it is also connected to the essence of all others and the world. Your soul self practices the other three principles: it pays attention to what is meaningful, has no judgment, and is not attached to the results. Therefore, your soul self is not affected by the criticism or judgments of others and is not attached to having things be a certain way. The concept of soul self is difficult to grasp because you also have an ego that interferes with your soul's way of viewing and being in the world. Understanding and strengthening your soul self will help you connect with what is truly important, putting your ego back in its proper perspective.

How does considering the difference between your ego and your soul change the way you think about yourself? Try asking what your soul would do in a situation where your ego is getting in the way.

Relationships

R ELATIONSHIPS ARE LIKE your garden. When you go outside and look over your garden, you assess how well it is growing. Are all of your plants getting watered appropriately? Are there weeds proliferating? Do you notice telltale signs of pests? We are regularly engaged in assessing and nurturing our relationships, particularly our more meaningful ones. You cultivate relationships by interacting and showing concern and caring. Sometimes a relationship is so strong and healthy that it needs little nurturing, but no matter how strong it is, it will not survive unless you intermittently assess it and determine what you can do to nurture it and keep it strong.

Does thinking about your relationships as a garden shed new light on them? Which of your plants might be in need of some fertilizer or pruning?

Gratitude

I T IS COMMON for someone to say, "I had a bad day," which can be very discouraging—especially if we have several in a row. But what does "having a bad day" really mean? Occasionally we may have a day in which it seems as if everything goes badly all through the day, from dawn to dusk. But almost always the truth is very different—that we had one, two, or possibly even several things go badly, and we generalized from those to the entire day, when actually the rest of the day went rather well. Saying that we had a bad day ignores all the things that went well, distorting and contaminating our experience, and making us feel much worse than we really need to.

Do you have a tendency to generalize from one bad experience? Think back on a recent day that you would describe as having been bad. Can you revisit that day and think of any positive things that happened?

The next time you have a day with many challenges, can you remind yourself that not absolutely everything is bad? How does doing that change your experience? Is it possible to talk yourself into thinking more positive things about your day?

Change

ONE OF THE frames of reference of people who are less likely to be depressed is that they have the sense that their situations are changeable rather than set. This is one way to create change. Search for the aspect of whatever situation you want to change that is changeable or start with the assumption that the situation is changeable.

Are you someone who makes monolithic assessments of your situation? Are things either great or terrible? Think about some challenge in your life and whether you can have a more nuanced view of it than you usually do. Does this way of thinking make you more open to the possibility that things can change for the better?

Change

I T IS OFTEN easier to change something small than to make a big, dramatic change. A bigger change often is not only harder to make but might create severe disruptions in areas other than the one that needs to be changed. A small change is less likely to cause such big changes or to spin out of control. In addition, if the small step made does not result in the desired change, not too much time or effort has been wasted.

What is the smallest change you can make in the area you want to change?

What is the shortest time commitment you can make that you think would make a difference and ensure you will stick with the change you agree to try?

Tell yourself: Today I will think about making one small change in one area of my life, and continue to make one more small change in that area the next day and one more small change the day after that, and so on. Does this seem possible to do? Give it a try and notice how much of a change there is after a week; after a month; after a year.

Health

S AVORING IS AN interesting antidote to negative thinking. It is completely impossible to be negative while you are savoring something. Savoring means being in total awareness of the experience. It is different from mindfulness in that it is an intentional, appraising awareness. This means that you deliberately select an experience to notice and you contemplate its qualities while you are in the experience. If noticing a sunset, for example, you can assess the depth and range of the colors and the moments of change as it fades, and you can pay attention to how you are enjoying it. You may be noticing your happiness or awe or interest in the experience and what it is like to be alone or with others while viewing it.

You can savor many things. You could savor the process of baking a cake or taking a walk. You could savor an emotion you feel. You could savor the taste and texture of food you are eating. You could savor the look on a friend's face or the moment when you awaken in a cozy bed. You could savor the feeling of putting on dry clothes after you have been swimming. When you savor something, you will have a sense of immediacy about it. Not only are you mindfully aware, but you are also having an awareness of how you are sensing, feeling, and thinking at the moment of savoring.

Take note of a pleasurable experience today as it is happening. What is it about the experience that feels good, and how might you translate that feeling into the rest of your day?

Mindfulness

IN JAPAN, FREE time and space—what we call pauses—are perceived as *ma*, the valid interval or meaningful pause. Such perception is basic to all experience and specifically to what constitutes creativity and freedom.

Pause is the prerequisite for wonder. When we don't pause, when we are perpetually hurrying from one appointment to another, from one "planned activity" to another, we sacrifice the richness of wonder.

Dedicate some time today to pause in your routine. During this pause try to take stock, to relax, to empty your mind—to do anything mentally that is different from the routine. Note how the fullness of this silent moment refocuses your attention afterward.

Could you permanently alter your routine to allow for moments of ma? *How might these pauses help you to become more aware on a daily basis?*

Stress

ONE OF THE most difficult aspects of anger is how intense and overwhelming it can feel; a lot of energy is generated in the body, and the physical sensations of anger are very powerful. After all, anger is an inborn tendency designed to support us in threatening situations. Some people believe their anger gives them a sense of strength and makes them feel good; they are afraid if their anger is "taken away," they will lose their power and energy. Of course, it may well give them strength for the moment, but there are many other ways to find energy and a sense of being in control of oneself while still being appropriately angry at the right times.

It is essential to remember that anger is an emotion that guides behavior, not a behavior in itself. Anger as a feeling is not dangerous or bad; it is an inevitable part of life. It is *how* you cope with anger that makes it adaptive or not.

The next time anger rises up within you, let it happen; ask it why it has come and what it wants.

Self-Awareness

I N APPRECIATING OURSELVES and choosing to focus on our
strengths, we begin to recognize our worth and value. People
who value themselves will feel better than people who focus
on their failings. People who value themselves will likely make
good choices in many areas of their lives, such as how they care
for themselves, what they eat, the amount of exercise they get,
and in their friendship and love relationships. People who have
a realistic and positive sense of self often are able to translate their love of self into love of others, expending energy in
humanitarian or other pro-social behaviors.

*Think about the choices you make in your life on a
daily basis. Are they the choices of people who take care
of themselves? Do you think about yourself as a person
of strength? Do you feel good about yourself? If not,
what can you do to feel better and make better choices?
Or would making better choices lead you to feel better?*

Problem Solving

HAVE YOU EVER been encouraged to just get away from a problem you cannot solve? As it turns out, this is a great way to get a new perspective and allow your logical brain to have a little space from the emotional brain. There are several ways to get away. You can get away by "sleeping on it" or letting your unconscious work on it for you while you do something else. Walking away from a problem can help you see a fresh solution that might have always been there or might be a totally new and creative way to resolve that stressful situation.

Today, try taking a break sometime from a problem you are facing. Directing your attention away from a stressful problem for as little as 10 minutes can give you a new perspective when you come back to it.

Relationships

THE IMPORTANT THING to remember is to give back as much as you take from any relationship. Be sure you are well matched with the friends you lean on, so you are not asking from them more than they are comfortable providing. And be sure to be there for them when they need some support.

Think about your relationship with one or two friends in your life. Keep track of your interactions with them over the next few days or weeks, attuning yourself to the little exchanges of assistance and support inherent in friendship. Is there an appropriate balance between asking for and receiving support? If not, what can you do to put things in better equilibrium?

Change

A N APPROACH TO changing patterns: Instead of trying to stop the pattern, introduce slight changes into it until you find one that breaks the pattern and makes the difference. Introducing small changes into the pattern is like introducing a small crack in the dam and watching the natural force of the water create a bigger and bigger crack until a large change happens.

Think about a pattern in your life that you recognize and would like to change. Can you break this down into small parts and try changing just one aspect of it? Does this one small change make a difference?

Mindfulness

THE BREATH IS a gateway to inner being, a bridge between mind and body. When someone is emotionally agitated, breathing becomes more rapid. Similarly, when relaxed, breathing slows and the mind becomes calm. Learning to work with the breath can become a valuable tool to enhance and promote emotional balance.

Breathing has profound meaning. Each breath we take puts us in touch with the universe. Breathing gives and sustains life, from the first breath taken at the moment of birth until the last breath taken at the end of life. Breathing patterns have the potential to promote health just as they can play a role in sickness. We are always breathing, and so it becomes an ever-present resource, ready to be tapped into when needed.

Take notice of your breath today. When does it tend to speed up, and how does intentionally slowing it down make you feel? Can you try to control your breath at certain moments to instill some calm during a turbulent time?

Stress

THERE IS A saying that in life "pain is inevitable; suffering is optional." Many situations may result in a feeling of physical or emotional pain. But that does not mean that you are *destined* to have pain or that your *identity* is wrapped up in having emotional pain. It means that at this time and in this place, you are experiencing pain. Unfortunately, this is something that people with depression tend to forget.

⟳ *Think about a painful time in your life that you managed to get through and realize that you were able to do it. If you are encountering a painful situation right now in your life, say to yourself: I am not my pain, and my pain is not the result of something negative about me. The next time you encounter a painful situation, say it again: I am not my pain, and my pain is not the result of something negative about me.*

Communication

SOME PEOPLE PRIDE themselves on never losing an argument. If this is a goal of yours, it's time to reevaluate. Rather than thinking of communication in terms of winning and losing, bear in mind that the real goal is for mutual understanding to occur. New solutions can be explored, and compromises can be reached. But if you are bent on winning the argument, the relationship loses.

When we argue with those we love, it is natural to dig into our own positions and defend ourselves. It is hard, and sometimes feels unnatural, to be open to understanding someone else who is making you feel attacked. The next time you have an argument, promise yourself to make more of an effort to understand the other person's position, and to focus on reconciliation rather than winning.

Self-Awareness

TRY SAYING THE sentence, "What else can I enjoy right now?" to yourself and notice how it changes what you attend to and how you feel in response. That sentence directs your attention toward what you can enjoy in the present moment, rather than the complaints and problems that so often occupy our attention and make us feel bad. Even in the worst situation there is always something to enjoy, so this instruction never contradicts your reality. And it also doesn't contradict any grumpy voice that is complaining about all the nasty stuff. It doesn't oppose it by saying "but"; it just directs your attention to other aspects of your experience, saying "and," joining what a critical voice might be attending to with noticing what you can enjoy. If you say that sentence repeatedly until it becomes an unconscious mantra, it can reorient your life in a way that is both useful and enjoyable.

Tell yourself: Today I will strive for a positive outlook and remember to ask myself what can be enjoyable at all moments of the day.

Problem Solving

ONE WAY TO describe most problems or unhappiness is that we develop tunnel vision, narrowly focusing on a problem while ignoring everything else that surrounds it. Expanding our field of vision to include much more of what is happening simultaneously in the moment provides a larger context that is literally wider and broader in scope, in which we see the problem in relation to what is around it, the "big picture" that includes much more information.

Think about a major problem you are having in your life right now. See how it clouds everything when you are deep within it. Is there any way you can expand how you see this problem to include even one small part of something new? Can you let a crack of light into the darkness that surrounds the problem? Does doing this lead to you to thoughts of a solution?

Relationships

AT WORK, AND in all relationships, it helps to be up front and clear about your needs. If you have found yourself becoming upset in the past when someone has not met your needs, think back to how you asked for your needs to be met. *Did* you ask? Were you clear? Some of us tend to let our own needs come last, feeling that we do not want to inconvenience others, and we end up feeling the effects of too much stress as a result. Others often *want* to help, but they don't know how if we do not tell them. So whether you need a quiet space in which to work or you need to feel more heard in your relationships, actually asking for those needs to be met is one of the surest ways to make it happen.

Do you have difficulty in stating your needs clearly? If so, why? Are you afraid that your needs aren't valid, or that people will resent you for expressing them? Make a list of two or three needs that you have, right now, that are unexpressed. Make a concerted effort today to express them. Notice the results.

Change

I T MAY SEEM paradoxical, but some people change by reclaiming or rediscovering their true selves. There is some debate as to whether we really have true selves, but most people feel some sense of unease when they feel they are not being true to who they "really are."

The most profound journey, I am suggesting, is to live more and more into your own life, into your own skin.

Close your eyes and relax. Try to empty your mind of any preoccupations about what is going on right now. Try to feel, deep down, who you really are; what the essence of "you" actually is. After a few minutes, open your eyes. Think to yourself: Is this me the true me, the one I express in the world on a daily basis? If it isn't, what can I do to change this and be more of my authentic self?

Mindfulness

ARCHERY WAS OFFERED to the youth of the warrior class in India to train their focus and acuity. Arjuna was a young warrior in training, later to become the main character in the *Bhagavad Gita*. Arjuna's class was instructed to draw their bows and aim for a bird perched in a distant tree to see who was the best. While the students held their bows taut, the teacher asked, "What do you see?"

The first student answered, "I see a field, some trees, and a bird in one of the trees."

The second student said, "I only see the tree that has the bird in it."

Arjuna's response was, "All I see is the eye of the bird." The teacher declared Arjuna the winner.

Are you comfortable with the way you direct your focus in life? How could an increased focus help you each day?

Stress

Y OU PROBABLY KNOW what it's like to live with extreme thoughts and feelings but when you pause, become still, you have an opportunity to experience two feelings at once— and to acknowledge the inevitable truth that at any given time you actually have more than that one feeling . . . you can be afraid and trusting . . . you can be angry and forgiving . . . you can be irritated and amused . . . . Take a moment now and simply be curious . . . as to whatever contrasting feeling emerges.

If you are feeling overwhelmed by extreme emotions right now, do your best to pause and be still. Can you try to separate out all the emotions you are having and experience them as separate feelings rather than just a single emotion of, say, anger or sadness or fear? How does breaking down your emotions make you feel about the problems you are facing? Do they seem more manageable?

Family

CONFRONTED BY A diversity of experiences, beliefs, values, and opinions, relationships get tested and individuals develop. It is, paradoxically, in the discussion around differences that much growth and change occurs, increasing the stability of family relationships. In other words, family members who disagree with one another and nevertheless stay connected in relationship end up feeling closer.

When family members see each other as people whom they love and completely disagree with, they must embrace a more complex view of themselves, their relationships, and the other members of their family. This increasingly complex view helps enhance members' curiosity about themselves and their loved ones, enhancing closeness and stability. The crucible gets stronger as it takes more heat.

Can you say to yourself honestly: I value and am thankful for the rich differences and disagreements in my family. If you can't do this, what steps can you take in your life to achieve a more open and supportive feeling toward family members with whom you might have some fundamental differences?

Communication

R EAL CONVERSATION, AND therefore real interchange, requires an exchange of experience. You talk, I listen, I talk, you listen, and so on. Both people invest in an intimate relationship, both people disclose themselves, and both people listen. We share our reactions to each other. We take risks. Together, we learn and develop.

Today, be very conscious of the conversations you are having and the give and take within them. Strive for a balance between speaking and listening.

Self-Awareness

THE ABILITY TO speak up for what we need and want is generally considered a sign of strength. When people say what they want, they reveal themselves and allow others to know them better. That act requires a great deal of self-confidence because to open up is to let others see who you really are, which involves a degree of risk.

Do you feel exposed when you speak up for your needs? Does this vulnerability make you silent when you should be speaking? How can you remind yourself that your needs are valid, and that only by expressing yourself can others really know you?

Problem Solving

PEOPLE OFTEN THINK of cooperation as the ability to compromise. Compromise may mean that, after some negotiation, I get some of what I want and the other person gets some of what he or she wants, however, neither of us gets what we really want. If I want Chinese food and the other person wants Italian food, we may compromise and go to a Mexican restaurant. While that compromise meets some of our needs (eating and spending time together), neither of us gets what we really want in terms of cuisine.

Cooperation is the idea that each of us can get what we want, although not necessarily immediately or at the same time. A negotiated settlement using cooperation skills may mean that we go to an Italian restaurant tonight and the next time we will go to a Chinese restaurant. Another solution might be to go to the food court at the mall where they have both Chinese and Italian food. Occasionally, we may need to compromise. More often, however, we should seek to cooperate. Cooperation works toward a win-win instead of a lose-lose.

⌒⌒ The next time you have a conflict with someone and start thinking about a compromise, try to think whether some sort of cooperation is a possible solution instead. Can you both get what you want from the situation, even if you don't get it at the same time?

Relationships

ONE OF THE best ways to enhance the social support you have in your life is to work on maintaining the relationships you already have with friends and family. We may think of them often or stay in contact via social media, but seeing them in person and creating new memories is important as well. Getting together with others is something we should all be doing on a regular basis. We may do this when we are younger and have fewer responsibilities, but it is a healthy idea to continue the practice throughout our lives. In fact, it is during those times when we have greater responsibilities and greater stressors that we need our relationships for increased support.

One of the surest predictors of long-term social and cognitive health is the degree to which people maintain healthy social relationships. Take stock of the people in your life and notice whether you actually spend as much time with them as you used to. Can you make any small changes so that you can reclaim some face-to-face time with your friends and relatives?

Gratitude

RECEIVING HELP CAN be initiated with the idea in mind that you are making it possible for someone who is interested in you or cares about you to show caring by helping you. To refuse help when it is offered may send the message that you are independent, but it could also convey that you don't value the offer of help. Furthermore, when you spurn a sincere offer of help, there is the possibility that you have denied a growth opportunity.

Is it hard for you to accept help from others? Do you feel it is a sign of weakness to express a need and let someone else fill it? No one can do everything alone. Think about an area in your life where you need help and make a promise that you will reach out to someone to ask for something. Even a small request can lead to significant relief.

Goals

IF YOU FIND yourself failing to meet your goals in a consistent manner, this should tell you something. Perhaps the goals need to change, or maybe you can gather some more resources to make things easier. If you look at each slip-up as a potential clue, and as part of the process of perfecting your new system, it will be easier to stay on track with your goals and even gather further momentum, rather than becoming discouraged and deciding to quit.

Think about a goal you have set for yourself that you have been unable to attain. Be honest about this goal. Is it too grand? Are you not really as committed to it as you say you are? Can your goal be reenvisioned in any way to make it more doable? Use today to focus on reframing a goal that has been a struggle with the hope that the new goal will be more attainable.

Change

WE MUST LEARN from the past in order to avoid repeating the mistakes of the past. We can also learn from our successes in the past. We must, however, live in the present. It is in the present where change actually occurs. The past cannot be changed. The future is not yet available. It is only through living in the present that we can change the future.

∞ *Say to yourself: Today I will focus solely on the present. I know that living in the present is the best way to ensure my healthy future.*

Health

PAIN IS A sensitizer in life. In running away from pain we lose our vitality, our capacity genuinely to feel and even to love. I am not saying that pain is a good thing in itself. I am saying that pain and the relief from pain paradoxically go together. They are the bow and the string of Heraclitus. Without pain we would become a nation of zombies.

Reflect on a painful situation. Did you learn anything from it? Did the pain, and coming through the pain, make you stronger? What lessons can you take away from that painful experience and how can you apply them to the future?

Mindfulness

B AD THINGS *do* happen. Yes, they do. *And good things happen too.* Living fully means embracing all that happens.

⬭ *During the course of the next day or week, make yourself fully embrace all that happens, both the good and the bad. If you have a tendency to focus on the bad things, make yourself recall positive experiences as well. If you have a tendency to ignore what isn't right in your life, force yourself to face those challenges. Notice how a holistic approach to life feels.*

Stress

WHEN OUR LIVES are relatively stress-free, a stressful event stands out. However, it becomes more difficult to recognize where our stress comes from as stress becomes increasingly abundant in our lives. We may be able to name a few sources of our stress—perhaps the most pressing and obvious sources—but we may miss some of the other, more subtle areas of life that are stressing us.

Becoming more aware of where the stress is coming from can help us to better manage it, particularly when we experience higher and more constant levels of stress.

If your life is particularly stressful right now and everything feels hard, make a list of all that is stressing you out. Notice how what feels like one big stressful life is really made up of separate parts. Even if the stressors are linked, they are not all from the same source. Does viewing them as separate make it more possible to see how you can manage them?

Change

CHANGE IS HARD. People get used to being a certain way and dancing a certain dance. Over time, those patterns become ruts. Some ruts become extremely difficult to change. At times we become aware that a change is necessary, and we may even make a commitment to change, yet we stop short of change. Few people change simply because of insight. People can know the terrible effects of certain chemicals yet ingest them anyway. Insight alone never cured anyone. The decision to change, an act of the will, is good but is also insufficient. Insight and a decision to change must be supported by new behaviors to actually effect change.

How often have you thought to yourself: I just wish I could change! How often has this wish been accompanied by an actual change to your behavior?

Choose one small thing in your life that you wish were different and for which you know what kind of change you could make. Promise yourself that from this day forward you will do something different to make the change happen, rather than just wishing for the change to happen.

Family

T HE ROLE OF parents is to give their children life, and then to give them the opportunity to develop a life that balances autonomy and intimacy while deriving deep meaning and purpose from each. In attachment-focused parenting, the parent uses the unique knowledge that emerges from her relationship with her child as a guide to child rearing. The moment-to-moment attuned dance that a parent and child find themselves engaged in is a source of enjoyment and delight, as well as a source of awareness and understanding about each other's thoughts, feelings, and intentions. This awareness is the best guide to knowing what is best for our children and for our relationships with our children.

Think about your child, children, or other loved ones. Think about their uniqueness as individuals. Can you make improvements in the ways in which you let their uniqueness, personality, and being guide your parenting?

Communication

S PEAKING TRUTHFULLY HAS to do with saying aloud the things that are in your heart or mind, and doing so in a way that is neither hard to understand nor inflammatory. It also has to do with only saying what you mean and meaning what you say. No threats! When we each communicate with skill, when we listen and speak with truth, clarity, and understanding, we create a safe environment in which both the individual and the relationship can thrive, and neither will be jeopardized.

It can be challenging at times to express ourselves in a calm and constructive manner. Have you had a recent communication that caused you to regret the manner in which you spoke? Can you repair the rupture your words caused? Moving forward, what can you do to remain patient and kind when talking with those you love?

Self-Awareness

SOME PEOPLE BOUNCE out of bed in the morning, eager to start the day, while others keep hitting the snooze button on their alarm, and then struggle to slowly drag themselves out of bed. The way you start the day is likely to set the pace for the rest of your day. If you start out eager and animated, it will be much easier to maintain that state, despite any difficulties that may occur later. But if you start the day discouraged, or in some other unpleasant mood, then you will have to work yourself out of that state in order to feel better, which is usually much more difficult.

What often makes the difference is what you first say to yourself as you emerge from sleep. You may awaken in response to an alarm clock, or in response to light, or to the sounds of others in the house getting up. As you begin to waken and sense the world around you, what are the first words in your mind? What was the first thing that you said to yourself this morning? . . .

How about yesterday morning? . . .

Now check several other recent mornings. What did you say then, and how did it set a tone for the rest of the day? . . .

Now notice all the tonal qualities of that internal voice—the tone, volume, tempo, hesitations, and so on. . . .

If you said something like, "I have to go to work today," in a discouraging tone, you probably had to work hard to get out of bed and get going, and that attitude is likely to persist during the rest of the day.

On the other hand, if you said something like, "Wow, which of my projects do I get to do first?" in an enthusiastic tone, then getting out of bed was probably very easy, and it would take a really unpleasant event to change your positive attitude.

Focus on the language you use to talk to yourself and notice what a difference it makes.

Relationships

THE ABILITY TO cooperate is like the ability to dance. Individuals have to know how to lead and how to follow and when to do each. If the music changes, dance partners need to know how to adapt by being flexible and working together to make the dance both fun and beautiful.

Cooperation requires making the covert overt. Cooperation means that each person puts what he or she wants out on the table. After exploring one another's needs, a decision must be reached. The important aspect of cooperation is not necessarily the final decision but the process used to achieve that outcome.

Are you a good cooperator? Can you put your own needs behind the needs of the group? The next time you are in a situation with others that requires cooperation, make a conscious effort to be a leader. Think of the musical metaphor you've just read and adapt to the changing music.

Goals

K NOWING WHAT WE want is often a difficult task. When people are asked what they want, they often begin by saying what they do *not* want. For example, "I don't want people to walk all over me." Focus on what you want. For example, you want others to listen to your needs.

Notice how you respond when someone asks you what you want. Do you respond by telling them what you don't *want? If so, pause before responding so that you can get a handle on what you* do *want. Be sure to articulate that clearly and directly.*

Gratitude

Y OUR AWARENESS OF gratitude might extend to include all the people involved in bringing food to your table or clothing to the store—all the workers in all the various phases of getting these essentials into your hands. You might begin to pay more attention to the service provided by store clerks, firefighters, teachers, and other people who serve the public. There is no end to the number of things that can go right in our lives.

The more aware we are of things going right, and the more we make gratitude a part of our everyday experience, the more likely we are to express generosity as well. Generosity and gratitude dance together and support each other. The presence of both depend on an open, compassionate heart, a willingness to share life's bounty, and a basic belief in life's abundance.

Make a point today to be grateful. Make a list of things for which you are grateful. At the end of the day notice how you feel about the day. Has the practice of active gratitude made you feel better about life?

Change

D ON'T MAKE TOO many changes at the same time. Avoid setting yourself up for failure by working on too many changes at once. It is usually not a good idea to change a lot of habits all at the same time. For most people, changing one or two habits at a time works best. You will probably be more interested in practicing some of the habits than others. Start with what you are most interested in, with what is most important to you. Recognize when you get off track and renew your commitment to practicing the good habits you have chosen.

Make a list of things in your life you want to change. Now choose just one of these things to change. Choose something that seems relatively easy. Do it! Make that change. Incorporate new habits. Cross that item off your list. Now choose something else. Choose the next easiest thing on your list. Repeat the process.

Health

WITH REPEATED PRACTICE, just about any response or reaction, negative or positive, can seem permanent. That is how anxiety disorders become rigid and engrained.

Conversely, this explains how new, healthier patterns of response can bring about and solidify change. In response to repetition, neurons can create new pathways in the brain for neural communication or rearrange existing ones, making it possible for us to continue to learn and change at any age. With repeated practice, we can retrain our brains to respond differently.

Oftentimes we don't even know that how we are responding to a situation is automatic. We must learn to exercise our minds—practicing new ways of response—if we want to see changes, just as we exercise our bodies to get the results we want, or to maintain physical health. Can you think of just one example in your life where you respond to a situation in an automatic way? Could you make a change to that and begin to break the pattern?

Forgiveness

E ACH OF US is the product of our past, yet we do not have to be prisoners of that past. If the past contains good things, embrace them. If it reeks of foul experiences, it is still our past and it has shaped us to be who we are. We must embrace that reality and effect change by recognizing the need for change, making the decision to change, and then implementing attitudinal and behavioral changes that support the desired change.

When you look back on your past, do you have mostly happy memories? Sad ones? Somewhere in between? Have you been able to accept those parts of your past that are painful? Is there a specific moment in your past to which you feel chained? What can you do today to loosen those bonds?

Mindfulness

MINDFULNESS IS A mental attitude and a way of responding to problems. At the heart of mindfulness is simple acceptance of your experience in each moment. The premise underlying mindfulness is that change can't occur when you avoid or suppress what's happening. Only by accepting each moment can your experience change.

Mindfulness practices teach you to simply observe the ebb and flow of your ever-changing emotions, feelings, urges, and desires, and to be aware of these states without judging them or trying to change them. Rather, in mindfulness you become open to what *is*.

Mindfulness is a way of training yourself to pay attention to life.

Promise yourself: Today I will welcome and attend to each passing moment.

Stress

WHEN MANY PEOPLE think about stress management, they think about how to cut down or control the stressors they face in their lives. But often we may find ourselves in situations where we cannot change our circumstances, or at least not right away.

This is why our frame of mind is so important—we can control our responses to our circumstances, even when we cannot control our circumstances. In exerting such control, we can lessen the negative elements of experiencing stress.

The next time you feel stressed about something, try saying this to yourself: I have control over the way I view my current situation, and I choose to acknowledge and let go of this stress I'm feeling. *Now try saying it again, and this time believe it!*

Relationships

WE CAN CREATE ideals for how to live: We can attempt to be attuned and open to whatever is going on inside of others, to be kind whenever possible, to be attentive and open. We can even have a notion to have self-compassion and be *receptive* to the many layers of our inner *self* that need nurturing across a lifetime, or a day, or a given moment or *mood*.

But life is full of breaks in these ideals, challenges to whatever we feel is a proper, correct way of being that we have not been able to achieve. Instead of beating ourselves up for the imagined or actual failures to meet these high standards, what we need is to *follow ruptures with repair.* A rupture is a break in an optimal way of relating to others, or to our own inner selves. A repair is an active effort to acknowledge the rupture and establish anew the *attuned* connection that serves to create *compassion* toward ourselves and toward others.

Reflect on a situation that disrupted your life emotionally. Can you think of ways to repair the break you felt either with yourself or with another person? Can you have compassion for yourself and reflect on ways you may not have acted as your best self? Can you extend that compassion to others?

Goals

IT IS ONE thing to want something; it is very different to come up with a specific plan to actually achieve your goal. It is easy to want something to change; it is much harder to make the change really happen. Like all of the other steps in recovery, putting together a plan sounds easy but can be harder than it seems. Goals can be so big that they seem to be overwhelming. It may be difficult to know where or how to start. It is important that each piece of a plan be small enough that you believe you can do it.

Are there any small changes to your life you can make right now that might have a ripple effect and enable bigger changes down the road?

Change

OUR CORE ASSUMPTIONS are so basic and so fundamental to us that we may not be aware that we have them. It is analogous to a fish not being aware of water because it has lived in water all of its life; it was born in water, breathes it, reproduces in it, and dies in it. It does not know water exists because it is not aware that there is a waterless place in the universe. Likewise, many of us have lived with our core beliefs for so long that we are not aware of their existence.

What part of your worldview do you take for granted? What attitudes, values, biases, and prejudices of yours might stem from unknown core beliefs? Can you possibly look outside yourself to see the "water" in which you live? Does this new perspective help you feel better about your life?

Self-Awareness

HUMAN BEINGS ARE meaning-making creatures. Our minds have an incredible capacity to wonder, hypothesize, be curious, and connect disparate experiences. We are constantly trying to understand and link the many events of our lives, and stories are a central way in which we put information together and make sense of it. Each time we tell a story we position ourselves in relationship to it. Voice, time, memory, and imagination provide us with all kinds of possibilities to make new meanings and place ourselves differently in relationship to a story.

How adept are you at linking the events of your life into a cohesive narrative? Take a moment to think about a familiar story of your life that you tell yourself often. Is there a way to look at this story differently? Can you position yourself differently in relation to what happened, as you tell it to yourself? Try reformulating one small story and see whether the new story gives new meaning to your past.

Stress

WHEN WE THINK about cutting out the things that cause us stress, we often focus on the biggies: the job that causes us endless frustration, the marriage that makes us feel trapped, or the financial straits that keep us up at night. But another way to relieve stress is to cut out the small stressors that add up to feelings of chronic stress. These are those little things that we are able to endure but that take a toll on our peace of mind: the annoying friend who can't take a hint, the messy desk that seems to swallow up important papers, the weekly commitment we always seem to dread.

Life coaches call these things *tolerations* because, as the name suggests, we simply tolerate them. We may not even pay attention to their presence in our lives, but we *feel* it. A common focus in coaching is to identify and eliminate tolerations and to work toward keeping them from creeping in and taking over. We all have tolerations in our lives, and they do take a toll.

Can you make a list of some of the tolerations in your life right now? What small steps can you make today to start working on fixing some of these or eliminating them altogether?

Family

THE PARENT-CHILD RELATIONSHIP can foster feelings of deep love and empathy, but it can also trigger self-defensive feelings and give rise to impulses that are "unparental." Loving feelings and trust are rooted in safety, in the kind of "felt safety" that is more primal and instinctive than the knowledge that you *should* feel safe. In order to sustain an empathic style of parenting, you have to have a visceral sense of safety as you interact closely with your child, both in times of quiet joy and in times of conflict. Love is a state of openness to another person, and it competes in our brains and bodies with closed states of self-defense. Parenting well requires the ability to stay open and engaged with our children most of the time, not closed off to them as we defend ourselves against feeling unsafe or insecure.

Are you willing to be vulnerable with your children? Can you take a look at your parenting relationships today and assess their health? If something doesn't feel right about them, will you have the courage to address it?

231

Self-Awareness

ASSERTIVENESS DOES NOT guarantee success. It guarantees that people give themselves the best chance of getting what they want. In the end, they may or may not get what they want. At the very least, however, they can have an assurance that they did everything possible to obtain what they seek.

Think of something you want right now that you do not have. Are you taking all the steps in your power to attain it? If not, what is holding you back? Maybe this means that you don't really want it. Think about whether that might be true and, if it is, have the courage to admit it. Otherwise, have the courage to go after it with everything you've got.

Problem Solving

HUMAN BEINGS SEEM biased toward noticing problems and when things are not going well. Perhaps it is a survival thing. If we didn't notice that tiger creeping up on us or hadn't smelled the smoke from a fire, we might have died during our evolution. To counteract that natural orientation, we can begin to deliberately notice what is going well or has gone well. Shifting from a problem frame to a gratitude frame can create change in our experience or may lead to the conditions for change in that we have more peace of mind and energy with which to approach problems and problem-solving.

Can you honestly say you have a gratitude frame of mind? If you don't, take some time now to think about a situation in your life that has bothered you for a while. Ideally, it should be a situation that feels overwhelming with no hope for change. Is there a way to look at that set of circumstances and see any good within it? Can you be grateful for any aspect of the situation? If you can find even one small thing to be grateful for, hang onto that and rely on it when times seem darkest. It may not change everything, but it may make a small change in how you feel and may lessen your feelings of despair.

Gratitude

EVERYONE AT EVERY age needs help at some time.

The acknowledgment of that need is noted in the saying from George Washington Carver: "How far you go in life depends on your being tender with the young, compassionate with the aged, sympathetic with the striving, and tolerant of the weak and strong. Because someday in life you will have been all of these."

For some of us, acknowledging that we need help is not an easy thing to do. If you are one of those people, take time today to try to accept help when it is offered, or reach out to someone when you are in need. Notice the difference this attitude makes.

Relationships

IN RELATIONSHIPS THAT work, partners are able to hold and contain the vulnerable underbelly that yearns for a warm hand and loving heart. Once partners are able to stay with each other through the process of uncovering and unblocking core emotion, as well as listen to each other's messages, the inevitable problems of living together as part of a family can be discussed and resolved. Repair involves a step-by-step resolution of issues, a process that can bind two individuals together as an intimately attached couple.

Ask yourself whether you are able to remain vulnerable with your partner, even in the face of extreme anger or discord. What can you do to maintain openness in the face of anger?

Goals

SOME PEOPLE USE the term *recovery* to mean that all symptoms are gone, never to return; some people use the term to mean *cure*. Recovery is the process of experiencing more in life than just illness. It is the process of going from being a patient or a client to being a *person* who may continue to have symptoms but also has more in his or her life than just being a client. Recovery is the process of finding out who you are, of choosing who you are, and deciding who you want to be, beyond your illness. Recovery is the process of having as full a life as possible, despite problems related to your illness. Recovery is having your own goals about what you want your life to be like, and then working toward accomplishing those goals.

What would recovery mean to you? How long would it take? How would you experience of life change? What goals can you set to help make those changes?

Change

THE INTENSE AND automatic reaction of the system to resist change has led to the development of various direct and indirect strategies, including the ability to laugh at ourselves and gain a certain lightness with regard to our own emotional reactivity. Humor is one of the most effective ways to detoxify and reframe a situation. Part of the power of triangles, ruts, labels, and rigid patterns is that they make us feel stuck, take the situation too seriously, and lose our sense of humor. A surprising and gently humorous redefinition of a situation, always without sarcasm, may jostle that inflexibility in such a way that the challenge is softened by an element of sharing. Of course the difference between humor and sarcasm can be a sharp edge and one must be very careful to carry it out with love and kindness.

Are you able to use humor when you need it? Can you lighten up a situation to allow some space for healing? This week, make a vow to use humor when appropriate to shed new light on a situation. Notice how this may lead the way to viewing things differently and with more sense of possibility.

Health

HEALTHY PEOPLE ALIGN how they think, how they feel, and what they do in a way that is harmonious and results in what they consider to be their character. These people appreciate that, whether they had a wonderful upbringing or had hard times earlier in life, they are responsible for who they are in the present. They neither aggrandize themselves for their strengths nor deprecate themselves for their weaknesses. They have a quiet, serene sense of self. They appreciate their strengths and acknowledge their deficits. They choose to focus on what is working without losing sight of what needs to be improved.

After reading this, can you define yourself as healthy? If not, what could you to do change your relationship to yourself to become healthy? Make a list of what your best friends would define as your strengths. Do you recognize these traits in yourself?

Forgiveness

I N ADDITION TO forgiving others, you can also forgive yourself. Everyone makes mistakes and will recall experiencing disappointments, shame, or self-condemnation for failure to achieve a goal, for an error in judgment, or for a harmful act. Errors of this sort can cause you to berate yourself and feel miserable. However, this kind of self-effacement, if it goes on chronically, can cause serious emotional damage including a lifestyle of negativity and regret. Practicing self-forgiveness builds insight and understanding about who you are as an imperfect person who lives in an imperfect world where mistakes and problems will occur.

Take some time to think of a past event where you wish you had behaved differently. Have you forgiven yourself for how you acted? If you haven't, what will it take to give yourself a break? Imagine that a supportive friend is telling a story of how you behaved. Do you feel reassured when someone else puts your behavior in loving context?

Stress

STRESS, IN EVERY form, deteriorates physical and mental health. That's why the focus of both hardiness and resiliency is to identify factors, internal and external, that enable individuals to digest and metabolize the stress in their lives. What happens in the process is that individuals engage more thoroughly in life and take responsibility for their choices. Consequently, the lessons of resiliency and hardiness make them more positive and able to problem solve in the face of adversity.

Are you effective at managing the stress in your life? If not, do you recognize how you may be letting the stress get to you and control different aspects of your life? Can you commit to certain daily practices, such as some presented in this book, to help you manage your stress more successfully?

Self-Awareness

PEOPLE WHO ARE assertive demonstrate a positive sense of self precisely because they speak up. They recognize that they have something of value to say. Speaking up in an assertive manner is one-third of what it takes for a person to be interpersonally mature. Another third is the capacity to listen to others. The final third is the ability to cooperate through a process of negotiation.

Do you speak up with as much ease as you listen to others? Do you cooperate in a group with ease? Balancing these skills is key to full social engagement. If you are less facile in some areas than in others, what can you do to even things out?

Relationships

S ECURE PARTNERS CAN tune into their loss of felt security, tolerate it, articulate their need, and risk reaching for their partner. This maximizes the partner's ability to respond.

Remember the last fight you had with your partner. Were you able to move beyond your own feelings of hurt to reach out to your partner? The next time you have a fight, can you make a vow to yourself that you will be the one to take the first step toward repair? If you do that, notice how good it makes you feel, and how much easier the reconciliation becomes.

Forgiveness

A FTER YOU ERR or offend someone—a family member, a lover, a friend, or even an acquaintance—and you want to repair the relationship, you employ forgiveness. The same is true for those who have offended you. Over your lifetime you will forgive others, but you will also need to seek forgiveness if you want to be happy. In the absence of forgiveness it would be difficult, if not impossible, for people to live together in harmony.

Forgiveness is, in many ways, counter to the competitive mentality. It involves considering the needs of others and even reconciling with others. Forgiveness promotes the needs of the group over the needs of the individual. It is inclusive insofar as forgiveness brings people together on the same level through the strengthening of positive emotional bonds. In forgiveness there are no winners and losers. Everyone's a winner and everyone gets a prize.

Can you let go of the notion of "being right" enough to forgive someone else who has made a mistake?

Identify one person whose forgiveness you have been wanting to seek, and think about how you might start that conversation.

Relationships

WILLINGNESS TO BE influenced does not mean giving in or "accommodating" just to make peace. It means recognizing what the other person has to contribute to a discussion or a solution and being willing to change something, learn something new from the other person, or adjust one's behavior or thinking in deference to the partner's wishes or better idea.

If it is difficult for you to be open to other people's ideas, promise yourself that the next time someone makes a suggestion you will listen with a truly open mind. Don't just give token acknowledgment to another person's idea, but really consider it and perhaps even try it. How does it make you feel to be more open?

Guided Visualizations

The guided visualizations and exercises that follow in this section are designed to provide you with more direction in your meditative practice. You may use them daily, in conjunction with the other meditations, or on their own. Unlike the preceding material, most of the visualizations here require you to take time out of your day (as little as a few minutes; as much as a half hour) to sit and practice.

Basic Breathing

RESPIRATION IS AN automatic function that can be altered voluntarily. What's more, changing the rate of your breathing, independent of any other activity, can change how you feel. Let's experiment.

Start to take quick, shallow breaths through your mouth, letting your upper chest heave. Notice how quickly you observe changes in your body. Your muscular tension increases, and you will likely feel anxious and uncomfortable. By accelerating your rate of respiration, you trigger the sympathetic nervous system.

When your system is stressed, your breathing becomes fast and shallow. As your heart rate accelerates, the body begins releasing stress hormones.

Now slow it down, breathing deeply through your nostrils, noticing the full expansion of your abdomen with the inhalation and its slow, even descent with the exhalation. Feel the wave of calm that washes over you. When you slow the rate of respiration, you trigger the parasympathetic nervous system.

Bubble Technique

CLOSE YOUR EYES and sit quietly. Imagine yourself floating underwater with a full air supply, with no tensions, and with no need to support yourself. Whenever you notice a thought, picture it as an air bubble in the water and watch as it just floats away and disappears. Continue with each thought until the water and your thoughts become very peaceful. This same technique can be used with the imagery of sitting on a riverbank and watching logs roll by, or sitting in front of a campfire and watching puffs of smoke disappear into the air.

The Horizon Symbol

THINK OF SOMEONE or something that has a very soothing
and calming effect on you. Visualize this image as being very
far away, just barely visible on the horizon. As you count backward from 10 to 1, picture your image gradually moving closer
to you. The closer it gets, the more clearly you can see it. At
the same time, you notice the calming effect as its presence is
nearer to you. At the count of 1, this person or thing is so close
you can reach out and touch it. Notice the effect of having this
image so close to and supportive of you.

Protective Shell

WITH YOUR EYES closed, identify a particular area in your
body where you feel safe and confident. Even if you don't feel
it now, think back to a time of feeling safe and confident; then
remember where in your body the feeling was strongest. Picture a color associated with this physical feeling. Now imagine this feeling radiating out from that spot in your body like
a beam of light. Let this beam spread into a "protective shell"
around your whole body. Imagine other people trying to hurt
you physically or verbally, but you are protected by your "protective shell." Experiment with setting the "protective shell"
aside or opening it a crack to let in someone or something that
you welcome, then closing it again for self-protection.

The Three Allies

BEFORE YOU BEGIN, think for a moment about people who have helped you as an ally in the past. Now sit quietly and take several deep, relaxing breaths.

Now recall a childhood experience when you felt particularly sad. Imagine the ally figure that we have been talking about. Picture exactly how your ally could have been the most help to you at that moment. Now focus inward and just notice the effects of the ally in your scene.

Repeat the same visualization, except this time recall a time when you felt particularly proud or excited. Imagine your ally responding to you.

Finally, repeat this scene with a memory of a situation when you felt very angry and frustrated. Imagine your ally helping you through this.

Falling Leaf

STARE AT A point on the wall across from you. Visualize a leaf at that spot. With each breath, count backward from 20 to 1 as you watch the leaf very slowly drifting to the ground. At 1, the leaf reaches the ground and you are very deeply relaxed.

Ten Candles

CLOSE YOUR EYES and imagine a row of ten lit candles in front of you, any style or color. As you exhale, imagine yourself blowing out one of the candles. With each successive breath, blow out each candle and let yourself become more deeply relaxed with each one. When all the candles are out, let yourself enjoy the peace and quiet of the room.

Positive End-Result Imagery

BEFORE YOU START, choose a situation you are likely to encounter in the very near future that you would like to handle more successfully than you have in the past. This could be an athletic performance, a public speaking engagement, an offer to use drugs, handling yourself in a family therapy session, and so on. Now close your eyes and slowly count backward from 10 to 1 on every exhale. Now imagine the situation in the future as vividly as possible, including sights, sounds, taste, smells, feelings, thoughts, and so on. Observe yourself, as in a slow-motion movie, performing the task successfully. Study carefully what steps you are taking to help yourself be more successful. Remember to make the accomplishment realistic—you may even imagine minor failures in addition to overall success. The more clearly you can imagine the successful performance, the more probable it will be that you can do the same thing in reality. This requires repetition and practice.

Stairway

IMAGINE YOURSELF STANDING on the top of a 10-step stairway, any kind you want. With each breath, count backward from 10 to 1 as you visualize yourself walking down the stairs, becoming more relaxed with each step.

Optional: You can continue this exercise by imagining that you have arrived at a special, personal place. Explore this place in your mind.

Visualizing Beyond Thought

IN THIS EXERCISE, use a peaceful visualization to slow down the mental chatter. Several scenes are offered, but feel free to use something that is personally meaningful to you.

Sit or lie down comfortably. Close the eyes. Think of the mind as a vast river and thoughts as small leaves or branches floating along. Watch from the banks of the river and allow the leaves and branches of thoughts to simply float past, with little notice except to observe that they do move past. Keep applying the same procedure: notice the thought, think about it briefly, but disengage from it and return to concentration as soon as possible. The task is to stay focused. Eventually the stream of consciousness clears, and no new leaves or branches appear as thoughts clear. Remain in meditation, watching the quiet stream. If a thought intrudes into consciousness, notice it, think about it for a moment, and then let it go. Return to focused attention: poised, observing the stream until ready to stop.

Another image that many people find helpful is a vista of grassy hills, rolling as far as the eye can see. The clear blue sky meets the green hillside. All is quiet, still. In fact, it is so quiet that you can almost hear your own heartbeat. The muscles relax a bit, without effort. The colors are soothing; the breeze is soft. Just looking at this peaceful scene, thoughts tend to slow—leaving an experience of calm and stillness. Do not do anything; simply enjoy the scene.

Experiencing Feelings

REMEMBER A TIME when you were experiencing a feeling that was uncomfortable for you . . . (fear, anger, whatever). And when you can identify that feeling amplify the feeling . . . let the feelings become more intense . . . just let those feelings come up . . . remember where you were . . . how you were triggered, what you were feeling and thinking . . . it is perfectly OK to let those feelings come up. Take all the time you need to remember a time when you were triggered and when you reacted too strongly. Bring up the details. Let yourself experience that time again, right now. Now step back and simply observe the feeling without judgment, without self-criticism or self-contempt for feeling this way. With acceptance, releasing judgment, like a detached observer, like a scientist observing an interesting phenomenon . . . just becoming aware and observant . . . being a kind of silent witness to your feelings . . . observing your emotions without reactivity or self-condemnation . . . And take a few deep breaths.

Now take some time to notice what it feels like to be calm again, to be calm and quiet just letting your mind become focused as you watch the developing stillness in your mind. That stillness will come sooner or later if you watch your mind . . . watch your feelings . . . and just attend. You can be assured that these feelings, even those that are most difficult, will soften, become less intense, less significant.

Be patient with this practice and sooner or later you will become more skilled and you can look forward to getting better and better at creating a comfortable shift in your style of reaction to thoughts, to feelings, as you engage in an ongoing practice that will help you settle down . . . to be more in control and less reactive to the inevitable triggers that come up in all of our lives.

OK Awareness

TAKE YOUR THUMB and forefinger of either hand and make an OK sign. Whenever you feel your thumb and forefinger together this can remind you that you really are safe and secure and that everything is OK right now. And it can be comforting to know that you can use the OK signal in the future when you need to remind yourself that you really are OK. That you do have the capacity to handle things in the moment. You can connect to this particular moment in time, enjoying sitting comfortably and acknowledge the indisputable fact that you really *are* getting through this moment . . . and, of course, you will make it through the next moment as well. And you can remind yourself that you really are OK right now. And each time that you return to this awareness of the present moment even in times of turmoil you will build your self-confidence so that if you experience temporary imbalance all you need to do is to put your thumb and forefinger together and acknowledge that in the moment everything is OK. Because it truly is.

Releasing the Panic

AS SOON AS you begin to experience that fear of losing control or that discomfort in your chest or stomach or perhaps a thought that something awful is going to happen, that can be a cue for you to take a moment for yourself that will support you. Mindfully, nonjudgmentally, just accept what it is in that moment. And I suggest that you begin to say these comforting phrases in your mind: "I am aware of the panic. I breathe through the panic. I flow through the panic. I release the panic." And in this way, you will let your body and mind express themselves and do what it needs to do . . . And you can be reassured and comforted knowing that all feelings come and go, they are time limited, fleeting, and will pass soon.

Tension Release

NOW IMAGINE THAT all that uncomfortable emotion is going into one of your hands. Make a fist with that hand . . . squeeze it tightly . . . feel the tension . . . magnify it . . . tightening that fist even more. Tighter . . . tighter . . . good. Now allow that tension to become a liquid in a color of your own choosing that represents the distress . . . worry . . . anger . . . or whatever the uncomfortable feeling is that you experience in your body. Imagine that your fist is absorbing all of the colored liquid, all the fear, all the discomfort. And then slowly . . . gradually . . . release the fist and allow the colored liquid to flow to the floor . . . to be absorbed under the floor . . . and further absorbed deep into the soil beneath the building . . . where it will be cleansed and released far away from you . . . far away from you. And do you notice the difference between tension and relaxation? If you like, you can repeat squeezing the fist and opening it again . . . noticing the difference between tension and relaxation once again. Perhaps you may be pleased to notice as well that the discomfort is diminished or completely gone and how good you feel.

Accessing Your Strength

WE ARE ALL made of many different parts, including a very young adolescent, an adult, or parts that are mature, scared, vulnerable, confident, and strong—so many different parts that reflect our developmental shifts, as well as our experiences. And it certainly makes sense that when you are experiencing fear, you can access a mature part, a strong part of yourself that can take charge of the parts of you that feel exposed or in danger . . . A strong mature part that can not only comfort the younger self but can take charge of situations in a reasonable way, a nonreactive way, a courageous way. Because you know there is a part of you that is always with you that is strong, that is balanced, that is mature, that is all grown up. It is always there, even if you temporarily overlook it . . . it is always there. And this is a perfectly good time to access that mature and evolved part of yourself. So take a minute to get in touch with that part of yourself that is adult, a part that is strong and balanced and courageous.

Now wait for the words that come from the wisest part of your being, that part of you that is most developed, strongest, and most solid, or even most spiritual. Or maybe images rather

than words will come to mind. Allow your unconscious to connect to that part of self that is wise and strong and all grown
up. And really feel it . . . your strength, your maturity . . . your
compassion . . . And with all those strong qualities . . . you can
look into the eyes of a younger, more helpless part and touch her
hand and reassure her that she's OK . . . that you'll handle the
rough spots for her. That she is not alone.

Identifying Disowned Parts
Projected Onto Loved Ones

IN THIS EXPERIMENT, allow yourself to review your relationships with family members, your significant other, and close friends.

- To begin, look for areas where you find yourself reacting intensely to any of these loved ones. Identify what it is they do that elicits your impatience, contempt, anger, hatred, fear, or sense of helplessness. Ask yourself the following question: if only they would change _____ or become _____ [fill in the blanks yourself], then I—or the situation—would be fine.

- Reflect on the descriptions you put in the blanks and then do the guided meditation on the next page discovering disowned parts to find out if you have projected part of yourself onto the other person. Chances are that *any quality that evokes an intense reaction in you points to a reflection of a disowned part of yourself.*

Identifying Disowned Aspects of Your Spiritual Self

- To begin, identify spiritual leaders you have known or read about who have a particularly powerful impact on you, whether positive or negative. You may also want to include friends or co-workers who express their spirituality in a way that has a notable impact on you.

- Pay attention to those people whom you feel have qualities you believe you could never experience in yourself and explore the possibility that they reflect a disowned part of yourself. Ask yourself if there were any childhood experiences or unspoken family "rules" that they conveyed disapproval of these qualities.

- Then ask yourself what is would be like to express those qualities in your own life.

Whatever you choose to do, remember that the journey into wholeness invites you into a level of self-acceptance that is transforming. When you know and embrace your whole self, both you and the world are safer for it. When you allow yourself to know your spiritual strengths as well as your vulnerabilities, the journey becomes more comfortable for you and those who travel with you.

Creating a Synchronicity Log

IN THIS EXPERIMENT notice the synchronicities that occur in your everyday life and then record them in a log or journal. In doing the experiment, pay attention to the smallest moments of surprise or "ah-ha"—as well as the unmistakable miracles or events that transform your life in unexpectedly helpful or meaningful ways. Make sure you also notice how, at times, you are in what seems to be the wrong place at the wrong time in ways that may be upsetting but still personally meaningful. You're looking for synchronicities of *any* kind.

- Once a day take a few minutes to write down any meaningful coincidences that have occurred. They may be positive or negative events or interactions that initially seemed random, or they may make immediate sense as being related to you in some meaningful way. Your goal here is to develop a habit of noticing synchronicities as they emerge.

- There may be times you want to determine how you may have caused—or could have prevented—a particular coincidence. That's a natural response. For this experiment, though, understanding the cause is less important than discovering the meaning a coincidence may have for you. Be sure to remember that there will be coincidences that seem to have no meaning to you. That's fine, as well.

• Over time, be sure to keep a record of how synchronicities coincide with intentions you have created, and notice how meaningful coincidences emerge consistently to support the fulfillment of the goals you seek to achieve.

Practicing Generosity and Gratitude With Money

IN THIS EXPERIMENT you have an opportunity to acknowledge and express gratitude for the money that flows through your life. As you become more grateful for this money, you can also remember to share your good fortune with others.

- Choose a particular day on which to focus your awareness on the money that circulates through your life. If an entire day feels like too much to tackle at the beginning, give yourself an amount of time that seems manageable. Then, gradually, keep adding time until you do spend an entire day with this experiment.

- Whenever you handle money, be it paper or coins, take a moment to acknowledge how grateful you are to have it in your life. In whatever ways you use it, allow yourself to be grateful that you have the money you need for the exchange at hand.

- When you get paid for your work, be aware of the reciprocity that goes on when you receive money for your services:

you give of yourself and you receive money in return. What attitude do you bring to the reciprocal relationship between what you offer and the money you receive?

- If you are someone who receives money for other reasons, such as inheritance or support from sources other than work, do you experience gratitude when the money flows into your life?

- Once you've explored how you acknowledge money or take it for granted, notice what it feels like when you give money away, whether you give it to homeless people, to charities, to family members, or to friends. Simply become aware of the feelings that move through you when you share money with others. Do you feel grateful to be able to share? Do you feel a sense of having less? There is no right answer here. Just become more aware of how you feel as money moves into and out of your life.

A Grounding Break

PICK A TIME during the day when you are feeling an energy lull. Sit comfortably with eyes closed. Begin by noticing your breathing and allow it to settle into a steady, comfortable rhythm. Then scan through your body to notice any unnecessary tensions and relax them. Sense how your body meets the chair you are sitting on and how your feet rest on the floor. Take the support from the chair and floor and relax into it. Note your affective tone and invite yourself to calm down if tense or to feel revitalized if tired. Trust that you can flow in harmony with your natural rhythms, and that in so doing, you will accomplish more and do it better. Take these brief 1- or 2-minute breaks periodically throughout the day. They don't take too long and will help get you back in touch with what you need.

Pond Relaxation

BEGIN WITH THIS visualization, and you will find your distracting thoughts clear away naturally. Sit quietly with your eyes closed. Imagine that you are sitting on the shore of a pond. The pond is alive with activity. Frogs croak; crickets sing; birds fly overhead; a fish jumps out of the water, feeding on insects, splashes back, and jumps again after a bit, in another spot. Wind whips over the water, stirring up the muddy bottom. All is movement. Then gradually as the day passes, the conditions begin to shift. The wind dies down. The frogs settle in for a nap, the crickets become silent, birds perch in the trees, the fish stops jumping and waits. The pond is quiet. The murky rippled surface calms as the mud sinks to the bottom, and the water is crystal clear, reflecting the natural surroundings. All is stillness. Then the frog jumps into the pond. Splash! Imagine this scene vividly. Stay with the moment.

Opposite Emotion

IF YOU ARE working on a problem with anger, sadness, resentment, or something else, think about the opposite emotion. For anger, perhaps it is compassion or love; for sadness, perhaps happiness; and resentment might be appreciation. The nuances of your own feeling will tell you what the opposite would be for you. Once you have a sense of the opposite emotion, imagine feeling this emotion in the situation that usually elicits the problematic emotion. So, if you resent someone in your life, what can you appreciate about that person? If you are sad about a situation, is there any happiness there? For example, when people have lost a loved one, they are often so overcome with the sadness from the loss that they overlook all the happiness and joy they had with their loved one over the years. By exploring the opposite imaginatively, much can be learned.

Opening and Clearing: Classic *Zazen*

ZAZEN, OR SITTING meditation, is the classic exercise for letting go of the moment in Zen Buddhism. Zen monks spend many hours meditating in this way, seeking to bring about an open, undifferentiated state of consciousness that continues to unfold. Follow the instructions carefully, and with time and practice you will experience a special calm and alert awareness. Attention is focused in the present moment, free of distractions while also being open and receptive. Brain patterns are both alert and calm, a unique state with positive long-term effects on the cortex.

Sit upright, cross-legged, with your hands, palms up, resting on your thighs. Keep your body and head upright and straight—but not rigid—without leaning either left or right. Hold your tongue loosely against your palate and keep your lips closed and teeth together. Eyes should be closed or half open. Breathe calmly and regularly. As you begin to meditate, clear your mind of all thought. When a thought does arise, notice it and then dismiss it, returning to your calm, clear mind. By continuing to do this over time, you will eventually find that thoughts intrude less and less and that your concentration becomes natural and profound.

Attending to Breath

TAKE A MOMENT to focus on your breath. You don't need to change your breath, simply notice it, and as you do, perhaps you can notice sensations that accompany your breath with a gentle curiosity. You can notice the texture of your breath, the rhythm of your breath, and even the temperature of the breath. And as you now take a deeper breath in and hold it for a moment, can you begin to experience a letting go of tension as you exhale? It can be such a relief to let go, can it not? Letting go, letting go of concerns, letting go of expectations, letting go of judgments.

Deepening the Breath

Now take five deep breaths, imagining with each inhalation that you are breathing in comfort and with each exhalation that you are releasing any remaining tension. Each breath leads you into a comfortable and pleasant state of relaxation. Each breath takes you into a deeper and deeper state of calm and comfort.

Attention to and slowing down of the respiration rate is a simple but highly effective way to calm the nervous system. Rapid breathing is associated with increased tension and anxiety reactions. As the respiration rate intensifies, the body is less able to take in oxygen. Conversely, slow breathing is associated with emotional equilibrium and parasympathetic dominance.

Raising Energy

THIS EXERCISE CAN foster the free flow of energy. Stand with legs shoulder-width apart and arms hanging loosely at your sides. Close your eyes. Make fists with your hands and tighten the muscles of your arms and hands lightly. As you do this, focus all your attention on your arms and hands. Notice the sensations; feel the muscles contract. Keep all your concentration on this alone for approximately 30 seconds. Then, let your hands open and relax your hands and arms. Notice how they feel—perhaps they feel longer when you release them. Pay attention to any sensations. Remain relaxed for about 30 seconds. Repeat this tightening and loosening five times, maintaining your mental focus throughout. If you feel able to, you can do it with your arms raised above your head, or extended in front of you, or extended out from your sides. Follow the same pattern of tension and relaxation, focusing your attention. Eventually you will begin to feel tingling or warmth in your hands, indicating that energy is beginning to flow.

Circulating Energy

ONCE YOU HAVE successfully felt energy in your hands and arms, you can begin to experiment with circulating it. When you feel warmth or tingling in your hands, imagine the tingling moving up your arms. Picture it moving into your shoulders. With time, you can direct it all around, especially to areas that need it for health and well-being. This exercise becomes easier with practice and works best when you are able to maintain your mental focus.

Unconscious Attention

HAVE YOU EVER gotten lost in a moment of daydreaming or reverie? This is a doorway into unconscious attention. Have you ever spent a timeless moment deeply concentrating on something of inner significance, then suddenly snapped out of it, realizing you had not thought of where you were or what you were doing? This is a form of trance, spontaneously begun. Seek a symbol that has personal significance and the potential to fascinate you. A mandala, an Escher picture, or any visual aid that is meaningful to you will do. Do not focus on it directly. Instead, let your thoughts drift freely as you look at it, allowing whatever comes to mind as you contemplate and focus deeply, so that your own thoughts and feelings can be stimulated.

It is positive and beneficial to be flexible and focused, with the capacity to pay full attention. Different types of visual organization can affect attention: diagrams, maps, and graphs can be objects for concentration, evoking your personal interest. Experiment.

Mood Shift

THINK OF A problem mood that you slip into repeatedly and would like to have more choice about. . . .

Now think of some music that might possibly be useful to pair with this mood, and hear this music in your mind. . . .

As you continue to hear the music, think of a time when you felt this problem mood strongly, and notice what happens. . . .

Then try doing this with a different piece of music, and another . . . until you find one that shifts your mood in a useful way. . . .

Then think of when and where this music is likely to be useful to you in the future . . . and then imagine being in that situation . . . and hear the music playing in your head in order to offer you more choice. . .

Troublesome Voices

ALMOST EVERYONE CAN easily think of a troublesome voice, but very few people take the time to really listen to it and notice where it is located in their personal space. The location of a voice turns out to be a major aspect of its impact on you, and it is one of the easiest things to change.

Listen now to a troublesome voice that makes you feel bad in some way, and notice its location in your personal space. Most voices are located either somewhere inside your head or in the space immediately surrounding your head. . . .

Is it located somewhere inside your head or outside? . . .

Is it in front or behind, left side or right side, above or below? . . .

And which way it is pointed—toward you, away from you, or somewhere in between? . . .

Take time to identify all these different aspects of the location of your voice. It may help to first gesture with a hand or finger to indicate where the voice is, and the direction it is pointed.

When a troublesome voice is located outside your head, it is almost always pointed toward your head. Now that you know the location and direction of your troublesome voice, you can experiment with some changes and notice how these changes alter your response to it. First change the way the voice is pointing and find out how this changes your experience of the voice. Notice if there is any difference between when it is pointing straight up and straight down. Or between pointing left and right. Or forward and back.

When the voice is pointing away from you, usually the volume is less, and your response to it is less intense. Most people feel better when a troubling voice is pointing away from them, and this makes it easier and more comfortable to listen to what the voice is saying.

Sources

All books are published by W. W. Norton & Company, Inc., New York.

p. 9   Simpkins, C. Alexander, and Annellen M. Simpkins, *Meditation for Therapists and Their Clients* (2009), p. 18.

p. 15   Simpkins, C. Alexander, and Annellen M. Simpkins, *Meditation for Therapists and Their Clients* (2009), p. 16.

p. 17   McMullin, Rian E., *Taking Out Your Mental Trash: A Consumer's Guide to Cognitive Restructuring Therapy* (2005), pp. 21–22.

p. 19   O'Hanlon, Bill, *Change 101: A Practical Guide to Creating Change in Life or Therapy* (2006), p. 96.

p. 21   Hernandez, Joseph, *Family Wellness Skills: Quick Assessment and Practical Interventions for the Mental Health Professionals* (2013), pp. 151–152.

p. 23   Hernandez, Joseph, *Family Wellness Skills: Quick Assessment and Practical Interventions for the Mental Health Professionals* (2013), pp. 104–105.

p. 25   Hill, Robert D., *Seven Strategies for Positive Aging* (2008), 91.

p. 27   Taibbi, Robert, *Boot Camp Therapy: Brief, Action-Oriented Clinical Approaches to Anxiety, Anger & Depression* (2013), pp. 40–41.

p. 29   McGoldrick, Monica, *The Genogram Journey: Reconnecting with Your Family* (2011), p. 21.

p. 31   Hill, Robert D., *Seven Strategies for Positive Aging* (2008), p. 132.

p. 33   Bruun, Elena Lesser, and Anne F. Ziff, *Marrying Well: The Clinician's Guide to Pre-Marital Counseling* (2010), p. 159.

p. 35   Stern, Daniel N., *The Present Moment in Psychotherapy and Everyday Life* (2004), p. 3, pp. 27–28.

p. 37   Shannon, Scott M., *Mental Health for the Whole Child: Moving Young Clients from Disease & Disorder to Balance & Wellness* (2013), p. xxiii, pp. 16–17.

p. 39   Waites, Elizabeth A., *Memory Quest: Trauma and the Search for Personal Identity* (1996), p. 271.

p. 41   Weiser Cornell, Anne, *Focusing in Clinical Practice: The Essence of Change* (2013), p. xix.

p. 43   Bruun, Elena Lesser, and Anne F. Ziff, *Marrying Well: The Clinician's Guide to Pre-Marital Counseling* (2010), p. 155.

p. 45   McGoldrick, Monica, *The Genogram Journey: Reconnecting with Your Family* (2011), p. 316.

p. 47   Hernandez, Joseph, *Family Wellness Skills: Quick Assessment and Practical Interventions for the Mental Health Professional* (2013), p. 123.

p. 49   Chenail, Ronald J., Anthony Heath, and Anne Hearon Rambo, *Practicing Therapy: Exercises for Growing Therapists* (1993), p. 139.

p. 51   Scott, Elizabeth Anne, *8 Keys to Stress Management* (2013), p. 15.

p. 53   Hernandez, Joseph, *Family Wellness Skills: Quick Assessment and Practical Interventions for the Mental Health Professionals* (2013), p. 178.

p. 55   Berg, Insoo Kim, and Peter Szabó, *Brief Coaching for Lasting Solutions* (2005), p. 18–19.

p. 57   McMullin, Rian E., *Taking Out Your Mental Trash: A Consumer's Guide to Cognitive Restructuring Therapy* (2005), p. 95.

p. 59   McMullin, Rian E., *Taking Out Your Mental Trash: A Consumer's Guide to Cognitive Restructuring Therapy* (2005), p. 213.

p. 61   Daitch, Carolyn, *Affect Regulation Toolbox: Practical and Effective Hypnotic Interventions for the Over-Reactive Client* (2007), pp. 90–91.

p. 63   Hernandez, Joseph, *Family Wellness Skills: Quick Assessment and Practical Interventions for the Mental Health Professionals* (2013), pp. 157.

p. 65   Abblett, Mitch, *The Heat of the Moment in Treatment: Mindful Management of Difficult Clients* (2013), p. xvii.

p. 67   O'Hanlon, Bill, *Change 101: A Practical Guide to Creating Change in Life or Therapy* (2006), p. 92.

p. 69   Rettew, David, *Child Temperament: New Thinking About the Boundary Between Traits and Illness* (2013), p. 45.

p. 71   O'Hanlon, Bill, *Change 101: A Practical Guide to Creating Change in Life or Therapy* (2006), p. 128.

p. 73   Diamond, Ronald, and Patricia L. Scheifler, *Treatment Collaboration: Improving the Therapist, Prescriber, Client Relationship* (2007), p. 302.

p. 75   Waites, Elizabeth A., *Memory Quest: Trauma and the Search for Personal History* (1996), p. 14.

p. 77   May, Rollo, *Freedom & Destiny* (1999), p. 89.

p. 79   Hernandez, Joseph, *Family Wellness Skills: Quick Assessment and Practical Interventions for the Mental Health Professionals* (2013), pp. 158-159.

p. 81   Gottman, John M., *The Science of Trust: Emotional Attunement for Couples* (2011), p. 14.

p. 83   Dinicola, Vincenzo, *A Stranger in the Family: Culture, Families, and Therapy* (1997), p. 14.

p. 85   Andreas, Steve, *Transforming Negative Self-Talk: Practical, Effective Exercises* (2012), p. 49.

p. 87   Gottman, John M., *The Science of Trust: Emotional Attunement for Couples* (2011), p. 16.

p. 89   Hill, Robert D., *Seven Strategies for Positive Aging* (2008), p. 132.

p. 91   Diamond, Ronald, and Patricia L. Scheifler, *Treatment Collaboration: Improving the Therapist, Prescriber, Client Relationship* (2007), pp. 275–276.

p. 93   O'Hanlon, Bill, *Change 101: A Practical Guide to Creating Change in Life or Therapy* (2006), p. 123.

p. 95   Weiser Cornell, Anne, *Focusing in Clinical Practice: The Essence of Change* (2013), pp. 14–15.

p. 97   Bobrow, Joseph, *Zen and Psychotherapy: Partners in Liberation* (2010), pp. x–xi.

p. 99   Scaer, Robert, *The Trauma Spectrum: Hidden Wounds and Human Resiliency* (2005), p. 252.

p. 101   Fish, Linda Stone, and Rebecca G. Harvey, *Nurturing Queer Youth: Family Therapy Transformed* (2005), p. 216.

p. 103   Hernandez, Joseph, *Family Wellness Skills: Quick Assessment and Practical Interventions for the Mental Health Professionals* (2013), p. 148.

p. 105   O'Hanlon, Bill, *Change 101: A Practical Guide to Creating Change in Life or Therapy* (2006), p. 57.

p. 107   Hughes, Daniel A., *8 Keys to Building Your Best Relationships* (2013), p. 35.

p. 109   Wehrenberg, Margaret, *The 10 Best-Ever Depression Management Techniques: Understanding How Your Brain Makes You Depressed and What You Can Do to Change It* (2011), p. 168.

p. 111   Scaer, Robert, *The Trauma Spectrum: Hidden Wounds and Human Resiliency* (2005), p. 289.

p. 113   Fish, Linda Stone, and Rebecca G. Harvey, *Nurturing Queer Youth: Family Therapy Transformed* (2005), p. 219.

p. 115   Scott, Elizabeth Anne, *8 Keys to Stress Management* (2013), p. 117.

p. 117   Guidry, Laurie, and Dusty Miller, *Addictions and Trauma Recovery* (2001), p. 105.

p. 119   Taibbi, Robert, *Boot Camp Therapy: Brief, Action-Oriented Clinical Approaches to Anxiety, Anger & Depression* (2013), p. 20.

p. 121   Scott, Elizabeth Anne, *8 Keys to Stress Management* (2013), p. 114.

p. 123   Watzlawick, Paul, John H. Weakland, Richard Fisch, and Milton H. Erickson, *Change: Principles of Problem Formation and Problem Resolution* (2011), p. 31.

p. 125   Napier, Nancy J., *Sacred Practices for Conscious Living* (1997), p. 87.

p. 127   Siegel, Daniel J., *The Mindful Therapist: A Clinician's Guide to Mindsight and Neural Integration* (2010), pp. 1–2.

p. 129   Napier, Nancy J., *Sacred Practices for Conscious Living* (1997), pp. 129–130.

p. 131   Simpkins, C. Alexander, and Annellen M. Simpkins, *Meditation for Therapists and Their Clients* (2009), p. 37.

p. 133   Costin, Carolyn, and Gwen Schubert Grabb, *8 Keys to Recovery from an Eating Disorder: Effective Strategies from Therapeutic Practice and Personal Experience* (2011), p. 224.

p. 135   Hill, Robert D., *Seven Strategies for Positive Aging* (2008), pp. 79–80.

p. 137   Andreas, Steve, *Transforming Negative Self-Talk: Practical, Effective Exercises* (2012), p. 83.

p. 139   O'Hanlon, Bill, *Change 101: A Practical Guide to Creating Change in Life or Therapy* (2006), p. 115.

p. 141   O'Hanlon, Bill, *Change 101: A Practical Guide to Creating Change in Life or Therapy* (2006), p. 39.

p. 143   Wehrenberg, Margaret, *The 10 Best-Ever Depression Management Techniques: Understanding How Your Brain Makes You Depressed and What You Can Do to Change It* (2011), pp. 253–254.

p. 145   May, Rollo, *Freedom and Destiny* (1999), pp. 165–167.

p. 147   Boon, Suzette, Kathy Steele, and Onno van der Hart, *Coping with Trauma-Related Dissociation: Skills Training for Patients and Therapists* (2011), pp. 264–265.

p. 149   Hernandez, Joseph, *Family Wellness Skills: Quick Assessment and Practical Interventions for the Mental Health Professionals* (2013), p. 75.

p. 151 Wehrenberg, Margaret, *The 10 Best-Ever Depression Management Techniques: Understanding How Your Brain Makes You Depressed and What You Can Do to Change It* (2011), pp. 121–122.

p. 153 Scott, Elizabeth Anne, *8 Keys to Stress Management* (2013), p. 53.

p. 155 O'Hanlon, Bill, *Change 101: A Practical Guide to Creating Change in Life or Therapy* (2006), p. 58.

p. 157 Simpkins, C. Alexander, and Annellen M. Simpkins, *Meditation for Therapists and Their Clients* (2009), p. 90.

p. 159 Wehrenberg, Margaret, *The 10 Best-Ever Depression Management Techniques: Understanding How Your Brain Makes You Depressed and What You Can Do to Change It* (2011), p. 204.

p. 161 Scott, Elizabeth Anne, *8 Keys to Stress Management* (2013), p. 118.

p. 163 Andreas, Steve, *Transforming Negative Self-Talk: Practical, Effective Exercises* (2012), p. 49.

p. 165 Andreas, Steve, *Transforming Negative Self-Talk: Practical, Effective Exercises* (2012), p. 65.

p. 167 Scott, Elizabeth Anne, *8 Keys to Stress Management* (2013), p. 107.

p. 169 O'Hanlon, Bill, *Change 101: A Practical Guide to Creating Change in Life or Therapy* (2006), pp. 145–146.

p.171 Simpkins, C. Alexander, and Annellen M. Simpkins, *Meditation for Therapists and Their Clients* (2009), p. 99.

p.173 Daitch, Carolyn, *Affect Regulation Toolbox: Practical and Effective Hypnotic Interventions for the Over-Reactive Client* (2007), p. 93.

p. 175 Fish, Linda Stone, and Rebecca G. Harvey, *Nurturing Queer Youth: Family Therapy Transformed* (2005), p. 20.

p. 177 Chenail, Ronald J., Anthony Heath, and Anne Hearon Rambo, *Practicing Therapy: Exercises for Growing Therapists* (1993), p. 125.

p. 179 Hernandez, Joseph, *Family Wellness Skills: Quick Assessment and Practical Interventions for the Mental Health Professionals* (2013), p. 85.

p. 181 Hernandez, Joseph, *Family Wellness Skills: Quick Assessment and Practical Interventions for the Mental Health Professionals* (2013), p. 125.

p. 183 Scott, Elizabeth Anne, *8 Keys to Stress Management* (2013), p. 125.

p. 185 Hill, Robert D., *Seven Strategies for Positive Aging* (2008), p. 106.

p. 187 Scott, Elizabeth Anne, *8 Keys to Stress Management* (2013), p. 178.

p. 189 Hernandez, Joseph, *Family Wellness Skills: Quick Assessment and Practical Interventions for the Mental Health Professionals* (2013), p. 201.

p. 191 May, Rollo, *Freedom and Destiny* (1999), p. 213.

p. 193 Wehrenberg, Margaret, *The 10 Best-Ever Depression Management Techniques: Understanding How Your Brain Makes You Depressed and What You Can Do to Change It* (2011), p. 247.

p. 195 Scott, Elizabeth Anne, *8 Keys to Stress Management* (2013), pp. 22–23.

p. 197 Hernandez, Joseph, *Family Wellness Skills: Quick Assessment and Practical Interventions for the Mental Health Professionals* (2013), p. 190.

p. 199 Hughes, Daniel A., *Attachment-Focused Parenting: Effective Strategies to Care for Children* (2009), p. 8.

p. 201 Bruun, Elena Lesser, and Anne F. Ziff, *Marrying Well: The Clinician's Guide to Pre-Marital Counseling* (2010), p. 157.

p. 203 Andreas, Steve, *Transforming Negative Self-Talk: Practical, Effective Exercises* (2012), p. 73.

p. 205 Hernandez, Joseph, *Family Wellness Skills: Quick Assessment and Practical Interventions for the Mental Health Professionals* (2013), pp. 141–142.

p. 207 Hernandez, Joseph, *Family Wellness Skills: Quick Assessment and Practical Interventions for the Mental Health Professionals* (2013), p. 39.

p. 209 Napier, Nancy J., *Sacred Practices for Conscious Living* (1997), p. 130.

p. 211 Diamond, Ronald, and Patricia L. Scheifler, *Treatment Collaboration: Improving the Therapist, Prescriber, Client Relationship* (2007), pp. 292–293.

p. 213   Daitch, Carolyn, *Anxiety Disorders: The Go-To Guide for Clients and Therapists* (2011), pp. 210–211.

p. 215   Hernandez, Joseph, *Family Wellness Skills: Quick Assessment and Practical Interventions for the Mental Health Professionals* (2013), p. 193.

p. 217   Daitch, Carolyn, *Anxiety Disorders: The Go-To Guide for Clients and Therapists* (2011), pp. 41–43.

p. 219   Scott, Elizabeth Anne, *8 Keys to Stress Management* (2013), pp. 80–81.

p. 221   Siegel, Daniel J., *Pocket Guide to Interpersonal Neurobiology: An Integrative Handbook of the Mind* (2012), {Entry 24, unnumbered book}.

p. 223   Diamond, Ronald, and Patricia L. Scheifler, *Treatment Collaboration: Improving the Therapist, Prescriber, Client Relationship* (2007), p. 278.

p. 225   McMullin, Rian E., *Taking Out Your Mental Trash: A Consumer's Guide to Cognitive Restructuring Therapy* (2005), p. 42.

p. 227   Roberts, Janine, *Tales and Transformations: Stories in Families and Family Therapy* (1994), pp. 71–72.

p. 229   Scott, Elizabeth Anne, *8 Keys to Stress Management* (2013), p. 103.

p. 231   Hughes, Daniel A., and Jonathan Baylin, *Brain-Based Parenting: The Neuroscience of Caregiving for Healthy Attachment* (2012), p. 13.

p. 233   Hernandez, Joseph, *Family Wellness Skills: Quick Assessment and Practical Interventions for the Mental Health Professionals* (2013), p. 94.

p. 235   O'Hanlon, Bill, *Change 101: A Practical Guide to Creating Change in Life or Therapy* (2006), p. 124.

p. 237   Hill, Robert D., *Seven Strategies for Positive Aging* (2008), p. 103.

p. 239   Solomon, Marion, and Stan Tatkin, *Love and War in Intimate Relationships: Connection, Disconnection, and Mutual Regulation in Couple Therapy* (2011), p. 33.

p. 241 Diamond, Ronald, and Patricia L. Scheifler, *Treatment Collaboration: Improving the Therapist, Prescriber, Client Relationship* (2007), pp. 271–272.

p. 243 McGoldrick, Monica, *The Genogram Journey: Reconnecting with Your Family* (2011), p. 343.

p. 245 Hernandez, Joseph, *Family Wellness Skills: Quick Assessment and Practical Interventions for the Mental Health Professionals* (2013), p. 17.

p. 247 Hill, Robert D., *Seven Strategies for Positive Aging* (2008), p. 114.

p. 249 Shannon, Scott M., *Mental Health for the Whole Child: Moving Young Clients from Disease & Disorder to Balance & Wellness* (2013), p. 52.

p. 251 Hernandez, Joseph, *Family Wellness Skills: Quick Assessment and Practical Interventions for the Mental Health Professionals* (2013), p. 88.

p. 253 Kerman, Michael, ed., *Clinical Pearls of Wisdom: 21 Leading Therapists Offer Their Key Insights* (2009), p. 136.

p. 255 Hill, Robert D., *Seven Strategies for Positive Aging* (2008), p. 113.

p. 257 Bruun, Elena Lesser, and Anne F. Ziff, *Marrying Well: The Clinician's Guide to Pre-Marital Counseling* (2010), p. 198.

p. 263 Goldberg, Louise, *Yoga Therapy for Children with Autism and Special Needs* (2013), 48–49.

p. 265 Wexler, David B., *The PRISM Workbook: A Program for Innovative Self-Management* (1991), p. 71.

p. 267 Wexler, David B., *The PRISM Workbook: A Program for Innovative Self-Management* (1991), p. 67.

p. 269 Wexler, David B., *The PRISM Workbook: A Program for Innovative Self-Management* (1991), p. 47.

p. 271 Wexler, David B., *The PRISM Workbook: A Program for Innovative Self-Management* (1991), p. 19.

p. 273 Wexler, David B., *The PRISM Workbook: A Program for Innovative Self-Management* (1991), p. 11.

p. 275   Wexler, David B., *The PRISM Workbook: A Program for Innovative Self-Management* (1991), p. 17.

p. 277   Wexler, David B., *The PRISM Workbook: A Program for Innovative Self-Management* (1991), p. 69.

p. 279   Wexler, David B., *The PRISM Workbook: A Program for Innovative Self-Management* (1991), p. 7.

p. 281   Simpkins, C. Alexander, and Annellen M. Simpkins, *Meditation for Therapists and Their Clients* (2009), p. 164.

p. 283   Daitch, Carolyn, *Affect Regulation Toolbox: Practical and Effective Hypnotic Interventions for the Over-Reactive Client* (2007), p. 81.

p. 285   Daitch, Carolyn, *Affect Regulation Toolbox: Practical and Effective Hypnotic Interventions for the Over-Reactive Client* (2007), p. 85.

p. 287   Daitch, Carolyn, *Affect Regulation Toolbox: Practical and Effective Hypnotic Interventions for the Over-Reactive Client* (2007), p. 164.

p. 289   Daitch, Carolyn, *Affect Regulation Toolbox: Practical and Effective Hypnotic Interventions for the Over-Reactive Client* (2007), p. 88.

p. 291   Daitch, Carolyn, *Affect Regulation Toolbox: Practical and Effective Hypnotic Interventions for the Over-Reactive Client* (2007), p. 173.

p. 293   Napier, Nancy J., *Sacred Practices for Conscious Living* (1997), p. 37, 44.

p. 295   Napier, Nancy J., *Sacred Practices for Conscious Living* (1997), p. 197.

p. 297   Napier, Nancy J., *Sacred Practices for Conscious Living* (1997), pp. 147–148.

p. 299   Simpkins, C. Alexander, and Annellen M. Simpkins, *The Dao of Neuroscience* (2010), p. 211.

p. 301   Simpkins, C. Alexander, and Annellen M. Simpkins, *The Dao of Neuroscience* (2010), p. 194.

p. 303   Simpkins, C. Alexander, and Annellen M. Simpkins, *The Dao of Neuroscience* (2010), p. 193.

p. 305   Simpkins, C. Alexander, and Annellen M. Simpkins, *The Dao of Neuroscience* (2010), p. 195.

p. 307   Daitch, Carolyn, *Affect Regulation Toolbox: Practical and Effective Hypnotic Interventions for the Over-Reactive Client* (2007), p. 68.

p. 309   Daitch, Carolyn, *Affect Regulation Toolbox: Practical and Effective Hypnotic Interventions for the Over-Reactive Client* (2007), p. 69.

p. 311   Simpkins, C. Alexander, and Annellen M. Simpkins, *The Dao of Neuroscience* (2010), p. 212.

p. 313   Simpkins, C. Alexander, and Annellen M. Simpkins, *The Dao of Neuroscience* (2010), p. 212.

p. 315   Simpkins, C. Alexander, and Annellen M. Simpkins, *Neuro-Hypnosis: Using Self-Hypnosis to Activate the Brain for Change* (2010), p. 84.

p. 317   Andreas, Steve, *Transforming Negative Self-Talk: Practical, Effective Exercises* (2012), p. 44.

p. 319   Andreas, Steve, *Transforming Negative Self-Talk: Practical, Effective Exercises* (2012), p. 11.

Theme Index